About the Author

Jack Chanek has been reading tarot since he was eleven years old, and he has been publicly writing about tarot since 2015. He has taught workshops on tarot, Qabalah, and Wicca around the country and is the author of *Qabalah for Wiccans: Ceremonial Magic on the Pagan Path*. Jack has appeared on *Seeking Witchcraft*, *The Magic Monday Podcast*, and *The Witching Hour with Patti Negri*, as well as teaching at festivals such as Free Spirit Gathering and LlewellynCon. He lives in New Jersey, where he works as an academic philosopher specializing in Immanuel Kant's philosophy of science. He can be found online at https://JackOfWandsTarot.wordpress.com.

Use the Cards to
Find Answers to
Everyday Questions

TAROT
for
REAL LIFE

Llewellyn Publications
Woodbury, Minnesota

JACK
CHANEK

FIRST EDITION
First Printing, 2022

Book design by Samantha Peterson
Cover art by Lucie Rice
Cover design by Kevin R. Brown
Rosetta Tarot ©2011 on page 14 by M. M. Meleen, creator of Rosetta, Tabula Mundi, and Pharos Tarot
Tarot card illustrations are based on those contained in The Pictorial Key to the Tarot by Arthur Edward Waite, published by William Rider & Son Ltd., London, 1911
Tarot of Marseille on page 13 used with permission of LoScarabeo, s.r.l.
Tarot spreads and image on page 108 by Llewellyn Art Department

Llewellyn Publications is a registered trademark of Llewellyn Worldwide Ltd.

Library of Congress Cataloging-in-Publication Data
Names: Chanek, Jack, author.
Title: Tarot for real life : use the cards to find answers to everyday questions / Jack Chanek.
Description: First edition. | Woodbury, Minnesota : Llewellyn Publications, 2022. | Summary: "This book is like a wise companion on your daily adventures, showing you the possibilities awaiting in every tarot card" —Provided by publisher.
Identifiers: LCCN 2022002817 (print) | LCCN 2022002818 (ebook) | ISBN 9780738769479 | ISBN 9780738769714 (ebook)
Subjects: LCSH: Tarot.
Classification: LCC BF1879.T2 C41355 2022 (print) | LCC BF1879.T2 (ebook) | DDC 133.3/2424—dc23/eng/20220208
LC record available at https://lccn.loc.gov/2022002817
LC ebook record available at https://lccn.loc.gov/2022002818

Llewellyn Publications
A Division of Llewellyn Worldwide Ltd.
2143 Wooddale Drive
Woodbury, MN 55125-2989
www.llewellyn.com

Printed in the United States of America

For my father.

Contents

Contents

Part III: Emotional

Part IV: Aspirational

Part V: Personal

Part VI: The Big Picture

Cards

Cards

Acknowledgments

I am extraordinarily grateful to the entire Llewellyn team for helping to put this book together. Thanks are due first and foremost to Barbara Moore, my wonderful acquisitions editor, who helped me turn the seed of a concept into a full book. Nicole Borneman, my production editor, helped to untangle my writing and make it readable for people who don't live inside my head. She is far more parsimonious with commas than I am, and the book benefited enormously from her critical eye. Lucie Rice designed the cover and did a beautiful job with the core concept I asked her to convey: that tarot is something anyone can do sitting at the kitchen table with a cup of coffee. Terry Lohmann handled the business side of things, and Heather Greene is perhaps responsible for me deciding to write this book in the first place. Finally, I offer my gratitude to all of the Llewellyn staff who worked on this book in its various stages, but with whom I never had the opportunity to interact directly.

M. M. Meleen graciously gave permission for me to use card images from the *Rosetta Tarot*, one of her stunning Thoth-inspired decks. If you like the card images displayed on page 14 or you are interested in exploring Thoth symbolism, I cannot recommend her work highly enough.

I am forever indebted to the authors, mentors, friends, and fellow readers who helped to shape me as a tarot reader. To all of the friends who whiled away the hours with me on the Aeclectic Tarot Forum, I am grateful for the insights you shared. To the members of the American Tarot Association, the

Acknowledgments

Free Tarot Network, and the Free Reading Network, thank you for the experience you provided and the opportunity to read for people I would never have encountered otherwise. Special thanks are due in particular to Benebell Wen, who has been a mentor and a friend. Benebell is the model of everything I aspire to be as a tarot reader, and it was at her encouragement that I began publicly writing about tarot so many years ago.

Finally, I could not have written this book without the support of my family, biological and otherwise. Thanks to my parents, who bought me my first tarot deck, and to my aunt Sarah, who promises that she is the most enthusiastic reader of my books. Thanks to the members of my coven, who are a source of continual laughter and love—and who let me read for them whenever the occasion arises. Deborah Lipp and I often find ourselves sucked into deep conversations about tarot symbolism and its application, and those conversations have opened my eyes to new perspectives on tarot that I might never have considered without Deborah's influence. Last but most certainly not least, Shane Mason is perhaps even more excited about this book than I am. Thank you for your unwavering love and support. My world is a thousand times brighter for having you in it.

Preface

I started reading tarot when I was eleven years old. I grew up watching James Bond movies with my parents, and one of Bond's adventures—1973's *Live and Let Die*—stars Jane Seymour as an enigmatic fortune-teller named Solitaire, who starts the movie in service of the villain before she's won over to Bond's side. As a child, I was captivated by her presence and her power. She uses tarot to predict Bond's movements throughout the film, to warn him about a double agent in his midst, and even to foretell her own love affair with Bond. She's a mysterious, enthralling figure. From a very young age, I knew that I wanted to grow up to be like her.

So for my eleventh birthday, I asked my parents for a tarot deck. My father rolled his eyes, but my mother had briefly flirted with tarot when she was in college, and the request was deemed harmless enough. When we went to buy my first deck, the clerk at Barnes & Noble informed me with the utmost seriousness that the cards would only work if they were given to me as a gift and if I kept them wrapped in black silk. I didn't have any black silk on hand, but I had a yellow polyester handkerchief that had come with a Magic Tricks for Kids kit, so I used that and decided it was close enough. In all my years of tarot, I have still never acquired a piece of silk in any color, and almost every deck I've used has been one I bought for myself. I've certainly never found that tarot stopped working because I bought a deck with my own money or stored the cards in the wrong way.

The readings I did in those early days were simple, unsophisticated, and often flat-out wrong. It would be several years before I was actually any good at tarot, but I read with enthusiasm, drawing cards for every question I could think of and looking up their meanings in the little white booklet that had come with the deck. I was entranced by the cards and knew that this was something I wanted to do, even if I didn't yet have the skills to do it well. About a year after I'd acquired my first deck, our house was burgled. The burglar, presumably in a hurry, saw a parcel wrapped in cloth and assumed it must be something valuable. He absconded with my tarot cards—and so my adventure with tarot was put on pause.

Some time later, while I was on vacation with my parents in the French Caribbean, something at a newsstand caught my eye: a small, unassuming red box with a white label reading *Jeu de Tarot*. This wasn't a tarot deck in the sense I was familiar with. The cards weren't illustrated and didn't have titles. The packaging didn't promise to unlock the secrets of the universe or give me impossible foreknowledge of things to come. It was just a set of seventy-eight playing cards used for the game of French tarot, like a poker deck with extra cards. Nonetheless, I bought it for eight euros, brought it home with me, and began to study tarot in earnest once more.

Learning tarot from this deck was an incredible challenge. So much of the language of tarot is visual, telling stories through imagery and symbolism, but I didn't have that available to me. Instead, I had to rely heavily on tarot books, taking notes in a journal, and trying to memorize the individual meaning of every card. I learned to use nonvisual information about the deck, things like a card's suit or number, in order to compensate for the lack of imagery. Later, I bought other decks and learned how to incorporate card illustrations into my readings, but my first years of serious tarot reading were all done with that unillustrated *Jeu de Tarot*.

Slowly, over time, reading tarot got easier. I'd lay out the cards and have a sense—some deep, inexplicable gut feeling—of how they fit together and what story they were trying to tell. Somewhere along the line, a transformation occurred: I became a tarot reader.

When I first started out with tarot, my parents had expected it to be a phase, something I'd obsess over for a month and then drop as I moved on to the next exciting thing. As it turns out, they couldn't have been more wrong.

Tarot has become a lifelong passion for me. In real life, tarot isn't what my eleven-year-old self had expected it to be; in fact, it's so much more. It has surprised me and challenged me at every turn. Although I can't rival Jane Seymour's outlandish costumes or dramatic presence (and the cards have not yet led me into the arms of an international super spy), my experience with real-world tarot has filled my life with more wonder and mystery than I'd ever imagined it could.

This book is my opportunity to share that passion with you. Anyone can read tarot given practice and patience, and it is my hope that this book will help you discover the same fascination with tarot that I found so many years ago.

Introduction

You probably already have at least some vague idea of what tarot is. Maybe you have a mental image of the psychic shop you pass on your way to work, an unassuming brick building with a neon sign in the shape of a crystal ball that promises you the secrets of your future for only twenty dollars per session. Maybe you've had your cards read before at a Halloween party or by an ex-lover and you were surprised at how accurate and insightful your reading was. Or maybe you have no prior exposure to tarot whatsoever, but curiosity and a natural inclination toward the world of psychism and fortune-telling have encouraged you to research what it's all about. Whatever your background with tarot, you're here because you want to learn more. Somewhere in the back of your mind, a question has formed: *Could I learn how to do that?*

Many of us have a preconceived notion of what a tarot reader should be: a woman with dramatic eyeliner, dressed all in black, who refers to herself as Madame Fortuna and smells faintly of patchouli. Comparing that image to our own, mundane selves, it's easy to feel like we don't fit the bill. Despite a curiosity about tarot, we might find ourselves thinking that tarot is something other people do, an activity reserved for mysterious strangers in candlelit rooms. Surely, it can't be something done by ordinary people in jeans and T-shirts, sitting at the kitchen table with a cup of coffee and the morning newspaper?

The truth of the matter is, anyone can learn to read tarot. Tarot is mysterious, yes, but it doesn't have to be. Reading tarot is a skill like any other, and it's one you can acquire with study, practice, and patience. This book will set you up to start reading tarot and will give you all the fundamental skills you need to build a deep, successful tarot practice. You can be just as much of a tarot reader as the mysterious Madame Fortuna, and this book will show you how.

What Is a Tarot Deck?

Before we get there, however, we should familiarize ourselves with the basic structure of a tarot deck. Tarot is a particular type of playing card deck, consisting of seventy-eight cards. It is not ancient, but it is quite old. The first tarot decks date back to the late fifteenth century, when tarot first came on the scene as a trick-taking card game played by aristocrats in northern Italy. Although tarot was originally used for card games, it quickly came to be used for fortune-telling as well. Nowadays, although the game of tarot is still popular in some parts of Europe, tarot is primarily known as a tool of divination.

We'll talk later about the ins and outs of how divination with tarot works, but the basic process is this: each of the seventy-eight cards has a range of thematic meanings associated with it, which are derived both from established tradition and from the tarot reader's own personal insight and intuition. When you perform a tarot reading, you ask a question and pull one or more cards at random from the deck. You then interpret the meanings associated with those cards and stitch them together to form an answer to your question. This process comes more easily to some people than to others, but it is something that everyone can learn how to do.

The seventy-eight cards of a tarot deck are divided into two groups: a set of twenty-two *Major Arcana* (Latin for "greater mysteries") and fifty-six *Minor Arcana* ("lesser mysteries"). The Major Arcana are the cards we tend to think of when we imagine a tarot deck, the ones with titles like Death or the Lovers. The Minor Arcana have less of a place in the popular imagination, but they make up over 70 percent of a tarot deck. In some ways, they're actually the most important cards in the pack.

The Major Arcana deal with big, universal themes in human existence, things like balance, transformation, authority, and truth. The Minor Arcana, on the other hand, are associated with themes from ordinary, everyday life. In the Minor Arcana, we find cards dealing with interpersonal relationships, budgetary concerns, health, work, anxiety and self-doubt, creative fulfillment, and sexuality—among other things. In short, these are the cards that express the sorts of concerns we have in everyday life. Sometimes we want tarot readings to tell us about big themes like the ones found in the Major Arcana, but more often than not, people come to the tarot because they want answers about their ordinary lives: *Will I get the job? Should I ask her out? How can I get my boss off my back?* For questions of this sort, the answers are often found in the Minor Arcana.

Like an ordinary deck of playing cards, the Minor Arcana are divided into four suits. Each suit contains both numbered cards (Ace through Ten) and face cards. Unlike a deck of playing cards, however, there are four face cards per suit. In addition to the King, Queen, and Page (which is the equivalent of the Jack in a regular poker deck), the fourth face card is the Knight, which comes in between the Queen and the Page. The face cards in tarot are commonly referred to as the *court cards* because the figures depicted in them are all members of a royal court.

So, we have four suits with fourteen cards per suit. The suits have their own names in a tarot deck, but they're different from the names of playing card suits that you're probably already familiar with. The four suits of the Minor Arcana are Pentacles, Swords, Cups, and Wands.

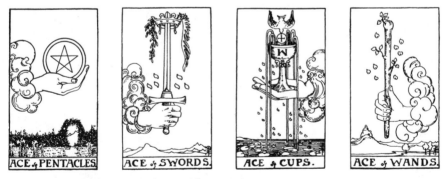

The Four Aces

There's some divergence between decks as to how these suits (as well as the court cards and the Major Arcana) are named, but this is the standard nomenclature, so it's what we'll use throughout this book.

All of this can be a lot to take in, I know. It can feel overwhelming to start learning tarot and suddenly realize that you have to learn how to interpret seventy-eight different cards and that they're divided in this complicated way. Don't worry too much. Right now, I'm just giving you the lay of the land. This is some basic terminology to help orient you and to start to break the intimidating monolith of tarot into more accessible chunks.

Practice Reading: Your First Reading

Let's set aside the structural talk for a moment and do a tarot reading together, right now. (If you don't have a tarot deck yet, worry not. Chapter 1 will talk about how to find a deck that's right for you. Return to this exercise once you have a deck.) Shuffle your deck and ask the cards, "What do I most need to know as I begin my tarot journey?"

Pull one card and lay it out in front of you. Before you do any interpretive work, take a minute to really look at the card. What is going on in the image? If there are people or animals, what do they look like and what are they doing? What sorts of colors or images are prominent in the card, and what emotional tone does the card set overall? Is it confident? Happy? Anxious? Fanciful?

Jot all of these impressions down on a notepad or in a journal. Then, flip to the page in this book that offers a description of the divinatory meaning of the card you drew. What are the main themes associated with this card, and how do they line up with the impressions you've already formed? Write down your thoughts, taking as much time as you like to explore this card.

Finally, read through your notes and think about how all of this information could translate to a message. You asked for advice, and your tarot deck gave you this card. What is the card trying to tell you?

If you pulled the Knight of Swords, for example, you might look through your notes and decide that the message of the reading is something like "Keep pushing forward and don't let your studies fall by the wayside." If you pulled the High Priestess, the message might be that the decision to start reading tarot marks the beginning of a new chapter in your life.

Try to boil the message of the reading down to one or two sentences, and write them down with the rest of your notes. Remember, there's no one right answer; the same card can mean different things for different people in different circumstances, so trust your gut and don't worry about getting it wrong!

With that, you have officially conducted your first tarot reading, and as far as I'm concerned, that means you now have every right to call yourself a tarot reader. This is only the first of many readings you'll do. As you work through this book, you'll learn how to apply increasingly sophisticated techniques to help you understand the cards, but the core process will always be what you just did: ask a question, draw tarot cards, figure out what they mean generally, and then determine a specific message that answers the question you asked. Everything else is just there to help facilitate that basic process.

The Suits and the Four Elements

One of the beautiful, elegant things about tarot is that each suit addresses its own set of themes and a particular area of life. The big, complicated tapestry of human existence is made up of discernible threads, and some of those threads are similar to each other in ways that we can identify. Breaking the tarot deck into suits is kind of like looking at a tapestry and pointing out all the red threads, all the blue ones, and so on; it helps us to deconstruct the big picture and see how smaller elements come together to make the larger whole. The four suits of the Minor Arcana identify four major themes in human life, with each card in the suit being a more specific variation on that theme. They are, so to speak, the four main colors that make up the tapestry of tarot.

- The suit of *Pentacles* is all about our practical concerns: health, money, work, housing, and all of the things that fill our immediate, physical environment.
- The suit of *Swords* is about intellectual concerns: thought, speech, communication, schooling, and mental health.
- The suit of *Cups* deals with emotional themes: love, friendship, family, intuition, joy, sorrow, and all other emotions.
- The suit of *Wands* touches on everything aspirational: hopes, desires, passions, willpower, and creativity.

This division of the four suits is based on an ancient metaphysical idea, dating back to classical Greek philosophy: the four elements. Ancient philosophers theorized that everything in the world was made up of four basic substances: earth, air, water, and fire. These substances were understood to be not only physical, but also to pervade the universe in a more metaphorical sense. The elements were thought to be the building blocks not only of all matter, but also of the human psyche.

Today, anyone who has taken a chemistry class can tell you that there are far more than four "elements" making up the physical world—there's a whole periodic table of them! Nonetheless, the idea of four elements as a basic division of the world is a useful metaphor, and one that has been retained in the structure of the tarot deck. See if you can find the overlap between the elements and the four suits of the Minor Arcana:

- *Earth* is solid, heavy, and immobile. Steadfast and constant, it is the embodiment of the physical world and our material circumstances. It also governs pragmatic concerns like money and health. A practical person is said to be "down to earth."
- *Air* is free-floating, quick, and impossible to pin down. Air is generally associated with our thoughts and fantasies. Someone who spends all their time thinking is an "airhead" or has their "head in the clouds."
- *Water* is flowing, receptive, and deep. It is the element of emotion, both positive and negative—just as we cry tears of both joy and sorrow. A joyous person is one whose "cup runneth over"; a mopey person is a "wet blanket."
- *Fire* is transformative. It can burn and destroy, yes, but it's also the basic spark of vitality. Elemental fire is associated with sexuality, anger, passion, spirituality, and creation. Someone with too much passion is said to be a "hothead."

Thus, the suit of Pentacles corresponds to elemental earth and the things that we *do*, the suit of Swords corresponds to air and the things we *think*, the suit of Cups corresponds to water and the things we *feel*, and the suit of Wands corresponds to fire and the things we *want*.

We'll have the opportunity, as the book progresses, to look at each of these suits in turn and examine them more closely, as well as studying each individual card in the deck. For now, though, you at least have a rough idea of what the skeleton of a tarot deck looks like. We have seventy-eight cards, divided into twenty-two greater mysteries (the big, universal questions) and fifty-six lesser mysteries (the everyday questions). The lesser mysteries, in turn, are divided up into four main areas of life, corresponding to the four elements. This breakdown effectively covers the whole range of human experience; whatever question is on your mind or whatever situation you're dealing with, there will be cards in the tarot deck to connect to what you've got going on. Whatever your question, tarot will have an answer.

How This Book Is Structured

To learn tarot, we're going to adopt exactly the same structure I've just described. In part I of this book, we're going to look at the practical, earthy side of tarot reading, and we'll look at the meanings of the cards in the suit of Pentacles. In part II, we'll talk about two of the more intellectual, analytical, airy techniques commonly found in tarot reading, and we'll complement that study by examining the cards in the suit of Swords. In part III, we'll turn our attention to the more emotional, intuitive, watery aspect of tarot, along with the suit of Cups. And in part IV, we'll talk about our fiery aspirations as tarot readers, our hopes and fears and obligations; this discussion will be paired with the suit of Wands. In part V of the book, we'll take an in-depth look at the people in the tarot; that is to say, the face cards from the Minor Arcana, also known as the court cards. To go along with them, we'll talk about the personal and interpersonal aspects of tarot reading. Finally, in part VI, we'll pull back and look at the bigger picture—the whole tapestry, so to speak—discussing how to put all of these skills together as a tarot reader. In that final section, we'll explore the big, universal themes of the Major Arcana. By the time you've finished reading this book, you will have everything it takes to be a skilled tarot reader.

Start Reading Right Away

Before we begin, I would like to emphasize one crucially important point that I wish I had understood when I was starting out in tarot. The best way to learn tarot is by doing. In fact, the *only* way to learn tarot is by doing. Book knowledge is helpful, and the various techniques and card interpretations given throughout this book will (I hope) be an aid to you as you begin to find your footing, but in order to learn tarot effectively, you must—*must!*—complement your book learning with practical experience. As with any other skill, like riding a bike or playing guitar, you have to practice in order to learn.

It's easy to be nervous as a newcomer and to want to hold off doing readings until you feel like you really know what you're doing. That's a perfectly natural impulse, and it's how I felt when I first started to learn tarot. However, it would be a mistake to let your trepidations get the better of you. I speak from experience; this is a mistake that I actually made. I didn't start reading, *really* reading, until years after I first began to study tarot. As a consequence, I knew a lot, but all of my knowledge was theoretical. On those occasions where I actually tried to read for other people, I'd find sweat beading on my brow and a brick sinking in my gut as I realized that reading tarot was a lot harder in practice than in theory.

Dear reader, I implore you: learn from my mistakes. Start reading tarot from the very beginning. Even if you feel like you don't know what you're doing. Even if you fumble your way through every reading, thumbing through this book to look up what the Four of Wands or the Ten of Cups means. Even if you feel the urge to preface everything you say with "I'm not sure, but…" Remember, you are going to struggle at tarot when you first start, just like you struggled when you were first learning to ride a bicycle. You're *supposed* to struggle. The only way to get more comfortable is to practice, practice, practice.

Over time, you'll learn how to ask the right sort of questions for a tarot reading, how many cards to pull for questions of varying complexities, and how to interpret cards—alone or in combination with each other—in different contexts. For now, the best thing you can do is acquire as much practical experience as possible. When you have a question, do a reading. Offer readings to your friends and family.

When you're just starting out, you'll find that you miss the mark sometimes, and that's normal, but there will also be times when you surprise yourself with how accurate your readings are. Read tarot often, and keep a record of your successes and failures alike; you'll soon find that you have an easier and easier time stitching together a narrative that fits the question you've asked.

And with that note, let's begin.

PART I

PRACTICAL

1

Setting Yourself Up

Tarot is an inexpensive and versatile habit. You can't read tarot if you don't have any tarot cards, but once you've secured a deck, you're good to go. All you need is a deck and a place to read. You can read on your own, at a party, or for another person one-on-one. You can read tarot in airports, in bars, and in college dorm rooms—I've done all three. There is no special equipment, locale, or timing required: you just need the cards and the person receiving the reading, who is commonly referred to as the *querent*. If you're doing a tarot reading for yourself, you don't even need another person; you can be your own querent.

With that being said, there are some considerations that are worth taking time to think about, especially as a new reader. While you don't need anything other than a deck in order to learn tarot, it's a good idea to lend some thought to the deck you're going to use, where you plan to read, and the sorts of study aids that will equip you to learn tarot as well as possible.

Choosing a Deck

The most important thing to think about is, of course, getting your hands on a tarot deck to use. It's possible that you already have a deck in your possession; maybe someone gave you one as a gift, or maybe you bought a new deck along with this book. If you haven't chosen a deck for yourself yet, the choice can be overwhelming. There are hundreds of tarot decks on the market, with all kinds of variation in art, theme, and content. What's the difference between them? Are some decks better than others? Which one is right for you? Having so many options can actually feel like a detriment. The following sections can help you get started.

Aesthetic Appeal

The most important thing when you're looking for a deck is to find something that appeals to you personally. When choosing a deck, look for something with artwork you like and images that you find emotionally evocative. If you're shopping for decks online, do a quick Google search and you should be able to find promotional materials with sample images of a few of the cards. If you're shopping in a bookstore, you probably won't be allowed to open up a box and look through a deck, but you can always write down the name of the deck, do some research at home, and then come back. When choosing a deck, ask yourself: *Do these cards speak to me? Do they intrigue me? When I look at them, do I feel like they tell a story?* If so, then you've found a great deck to use. If not, keep looking.

Remember, tarot is about building a narrative. It's a form of storytelling, and the cards are an aid to putting together the story. You want to be able to pull cards, look at them, and launch into "Once upon a time…" This is easiest to do when the card images draw you in and provoke your imagination.

Illustrated and Unillustrated Pips

Not all tarot decks are fully illustrated. In some decks, only the Major Arcana depict complete scenes; the Minor Arcana (often referred to as the *pips*) are more like ordinary playing cards. So, for example, the Three of Swords would simply be a card with three swords drawn on it, potentially in an interesting geometric configuration, but with no other symbolism or imagery to aid in interpretation. Likewise, the Four of Cups would just be an arrangement of four goblets, the Five of Wands would be a bundle of five sticks, and so on. Some readers prefer the simplicity of unillustrated pips, finding the cards cleaner, more elegant, and easier to interpret without additional images cluttering up the frame. For most, though, an absence of imagery in the Minor Arcana can be challenging because there's less visual information to help the reader connect to the meaning of the cards. This is especially true for new readers, who are still learning how to interpret the cards and who often benefit from the added visual cues.

Ultimately, it's a matter of preference, and if you know that you would prefer to read with unillustrated pips, then you should look for a deck that fits that description. If you're unsure, though, I would recommend starting out with a deck that has fully illustrated minors—at least to begin with. You'll likely have an easier time learning the card meanings and connecting with their energy when you have robust imagery to work with.

Schools of Tarot

While there are hundreds upon hundreds of tarot decks available, three stand out as the most famous and influential: the Tarot de Marseille, the Rider-Waite-Smith, and the Thoth. These three decks are so famous that they have become almost synonymous with tarot. Moreover, these decks are so popular that they have shaped the rest of the tarot world. Almost every deck available has imagery derived from one of these three, and together they form the three major "schools" of tarot.

As a beginner, you're not expected to know the ins and outs of different styles of tarot decks. How could you? But a brief overview here might help give you an idea of the direction you'd like to go when looking for a deck.

The Tarot de Marseille (TdM for short) is a historical deck from the early days of tarot's development. TdM-style decks typically have unillustrated pips, and the cards are printed in a woodcut style, as that's how the original deck was made.

The Rider-Waite-Smith Tarot (RWS) was designed in the early twentieth century by English occultist Arthur Edward Waite and illustrated by the Jamaican-English artist Pamela Colman Smith. Most tarot decks are RWS-based, and almost any tarot book (including this one) will give you card interpretations based on this school.

Also in the twentieth century, the Thoth Tarot was designed by the famous English magician Aleister Crowley, illustrated by Lady Frieda Harris. Thoth-style decks are loaded with dense occult imagery that can make them less accessible to the inexperienced reader. The Minor Arcana tend to be unillustrated, but Thoth decks do have the advantage of including keywords on all of the minors, which helps with interpreting the cards.

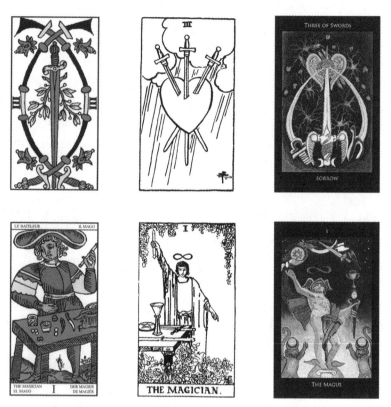

The Magician and the Three of Swords side-by-side in three decks: a TdM-style, a RWS-style, and a Thoth-style

You may find that one of these decks (or the schools derived from them) speaks to you more than the others, in which case, you should look for a deck with similar imagery. If you're ambivalent, I'd recommend starting with a RWS-style deck. The illustrated Minor Arcana are a huge help to novice readers, and almost any tarot book you read will have been written with RWS imagery in mind, which will make the learning process smoother.

Themed Decks

Some decks have artwork organized around a particular subject matter, theme, or art style. For example, there's an Edgar Allan Poe tarot deck, an *Alice in Wonderland* tarot deck, and a fairy tale tarot deck. You can find decks with imagery focused on fairies, cats, King Arthur, Halloween, angels, and more. If there's a particular artist or art movement you love, you can find Art

Nouveau decks, impressionist decks, and the like. If there's a subject you love or if you have a particular area of expertise, you may want to investigate one of these themed decks. Themed imagery can be familiar and accessible, and it can give you a point of entry into tarot that you might not otherwise have.

Unconventional Decks

Some decks deviate from tarot conventions in minor ways. For example, the suits of the Minor Arcana or the ranks of the court cards might be renamed to fit the deck's theme, or the elemental associations of the Wands and Swords might be swapped (that is to say, a deck might associate Wands with air and Swords with fire). Likewise, individual cards in the Major Arcana may be renamed as well. Some decks even add an extra card, providing seventy-nine cards in the pack rather than seventy-eight.

All of these changes are perfectly acceptable, and most tend to be fairly superficial, but they're worth keeping an eye on when you're considering which deck you want to buy. If your deck does deviate in some small ways from the general conventions of the tarot world, then you'll want to be aware of that so you don't get confused by other decks or the information you find in books and online.

It's Not "Till Death Do Us Part"

Finally, remember that choosing a deck is not a lifetime commitment, and it's okay if you change your mind further down the line. You don't have to read with the same deck your whole life; you're just choosing something to help get you started. If you decide, after some time, that the deck you have doesn't work for you—or if you like your deck but you just want to introduce some variety—it's okay to branch out and try something new. For now, you just need something to get you started.

Practice Reading: Getting to Know Your Deck

Once you've obtained your deck, take it out of its box and look through it. Examine each card and get a sense for how they make you feel, individually and as a collective whole. Are there any cards that stand out to you? Which cards are your favorites? What do you like about them? What are the defining qualities that determine your overall impression of the deck?

Shuffle the cards and ask, "What should I know about this tarot deck?" Pull one card, and interpret it according to the same process you used in our first practice reading. Begin by looking at the imagery of the card, forming a first impression, and identifying the prominent visual motifs. Take a moment to write down what you get from looking at the card. Then, flip to the appropriate page in this book and read through the interpretation I've provided. How does that interpretation align with your impressions, and how does it differ? Write this down as well.

Finally, try to synthesize this information into a message of one or two sentences. If this card is the answer to your question, how would you phrase that answer? What is the deck trying to tell you? It can be tempting to skip over this step, but the best way to get clarity about what a tarot reading means is to force yourself to articulate its message, either out loud or in writing.

Caring for a Deck

The practical aspects of caring for a tarot deck are straightforward, just like for any other deck of cards. You want to keep your deck clean and dry. Avoid bending or tearing the cards. If the cards stick to each other and are hard to shuffle, you can use a bit of fanning powder (used by stage magicians) to help them glide over each other more easily. It's generally a good idea to wash your hands before handling your deck, and to have other people do the same. Some readers don't let anyone else touch their decks, while others will have a querent shuffle, cut, or draw the cards in order to make the querent an active participant in their reading. Whatever you do is up to your personal preference, but you should make sure that anyone who handles your deck is showing it the same care that you do.

You may wish to store your cards in a special place; this can be as simple or as fancy as you like, so long as they're somewhere they won't get damaged. Perhaps you have a dedicated wooden box for your deck, or you wrap your deck in a cloth handkerchief when it's not in use. Personally, I keep every deck in the original cardboard box it came in, and I store my decks on a bookshelf. Do what feels right to you.

Aside from the practical care of a deck, there is also the more mystical side of things. Some readers like to routinely cleanse their tarot decks in order to clear away any psychic detritus that may build up from repeated use.

This is totally optional and depends on your view of tarot; if you take a more mystical approach to tarot, this sort of psychic hygiene will likely appeal to you, but if you're not interested in ritually cleansing your deck, you certainly don't have to. There are a variety of ways to perform a deck cleansing, and no approach is better than another; as with all things, it comes down to what works for you and what feels right. Here are a couple of different methods you may wish to try:

- Leaving your deck out on a windowsill every month to charge under the light of the full moon.
- Wafting your deck through incense smoke to purify it. (Rosemary, juniper, and cedar are all plants traditionally associated with purification, and would be well suited to this purpose; dragon's blood resin is also a great purification incense.)
- Ringing a bell over your deck to drive away negative energy.
- Placing a crystal on top of your deck to charge it, or surrounding your deck with a crystal grid. (You can choose the crystals depending on your purpose; crystals like amethyst, clear quartz, and selenite are all good for enhancing psychic power and charging a deck.)

If you choose to cleanse your deck, you may do so as often or as rarely as you wish. Some people cleanse their decks between each reading, others do so every month or two, and still others will only do so when they intuitively feel that the deck needs it. You can also purify your deck when you first acquire it without making a commitment to repeated cleansings in the future.

Keeping a Tarot Journal

You'll notice that in the exercises I've provided so far, I make reference to taking notes during a reading and writing down your interpretations so that you can refer back to them later. Ideally, it's good practice to keep all of your tarot notes in one place; that way, they're organized and easy to find, and you can look back not just at one reading, but at the overall arc of your progress as a tarot reader. This is why one of the most commonly recommended practices for new readers is to keep a tarot journal.

Your tarot journal can be anything: a composition notebook, a beautiful leather-bound book, a three-ring binder, or a digital document. Personally, I run a tarot blog, which effectively serves as my (semi-public) tarot journal—it's the place where I can hash out my thoughts on tarot, develop new card layouts, reflect on the meanings of particular cards, document my readings, and think about my life events in the context of tarot symbolism.

There's a chance that you're groaning and rolling your eyes at the mention of keeping a journal. Believe me, I understand. No one finds journaling more tedious and frustrating than I do. I've always admired fervent journalers, but I lack the discipline to keep up with the practice. Nonetheless, I must tell you from the bottom of my heart that it's worth your time to keep a tarot journal, especially when you're just starting out. I cannot overstate the value of having a record to look back on as you learn tarot. A journal will help you keep track of your successes, learn from your mistakes, and develop a progressively deeper relationship with the cards over time.

A tarot journal is a personal thing, and everyone's journal will look slightly different depending on what's suited to them. That said, here are a few suggestions for things you can include in yours:

- Keep a record of every reading you perform. Who was the reading for? What was the question asked? If you own multiple decks, which deck did you use? How many cards did you draw, which cards did you pull, and what layout (if any) did you use? Make note of the interpretations you provided, including any predictions. Later on, reread this journal entry once the events of the reading have played themselves out. Annotate it with notes about where you were correct and where your reading missed the mark.

- Take notes on each individual card in your tarot deck. Make note of the overall impression the card gives you, then focus on specific details. Write down a list of the major colors, images, figures, actions, and symbols found in the card. What do each of these symbols mean to you personally? How do they contribute to the overall feeling of the card? Do any of these figures, images, or colors appear in other cards in the deck, and if so, what's the connection between those cards?

- Take notes on the "official" interpretations of every card, as given by this book and other resources. As you study each card, try to think of a few different keywords to associate with it. Pay special attention to the places where your intuitive associations are particularly in line with the given interpretations, as well as the places where they diverge.

- Write about events that are going on in your life, then connect them back to the symbolism of tarot. Think about what happened to you on a noteworthy day, and consider how you express those events using themes from the tarot. Was your disastrous work meeting like the Ten of Swords? Is your new creative project moving with the speed of the Eight of Wands? Try to filter your ordinary, everyday life through the lens of tarot.

- Try associating tarot with characters and events from movies, books, and television. Which tarot card is Superman? What about Walter White? How would you explain the plot of *Romeo and Juliet* using tarot?

- Do an interpretive art project—drawing a sketch, writing a poem, making a collage, etc.—for each tarot card. Try experimenting with different mediums. How can you get your creative expression flowing and connect yourself to the cards in ways other than just writing?

These are just a few suggestions to get you started. There are countless ways to keep a tarot journal; the only limitations are your own imagination and creativity. Moreover, remember that your journal is for *you*. No one else ever needs to see it. Don't be self-conscious about getting it "right" or making it look perfect. It's okay to be messy! Cross things out, misspell words, and write down your thoughts about the cards even if you're worried they might be wrong. This is a place for you to experiment. The goal is for you to read back through your old journal entries after a year or more and say, "Wow, look how much I've learned since then." So don't feel like your journal has to be a picture-perfect tarot textbook. It is, first and foremost, a working notebook.

The Daily Draw

There is one other practice that's almost universally recommended to novice tarot readers, and for good reason: performing a tarot reading every day. The key purpose of this exercise is for you to gain practical experience in tarot interpretation; remember, the only real way to learn tarot is by doing.

The most common version of this is the so-called "daily draw," where you pull one card at the start of every day to see what your day is going to be like. To perform a daily draw, you would shuffle your cards at the beginning of the day, ask what's in store for your day, and then go through the process of interpretation that we've already outlined in the first two practice exercises. Then, you would come back at the end of the day and evaluate the accuracy of your predictions.

As an alternative, some people prefer to do their daily draw at the end of the day, once they already know what's happened. Doing this makes the interpretive process easier; rather than having to translate a card into a concrete prediction for something that hasn't happened yet, you can connect the card to one event from a finite list of things that happened in the day. For this reason, this version of a daily draw may be more appealing to absolute novices, and it's totally okay if you want to start out this way in order to get your feet wet. However, if you do, don't let this be the be-all and end-all of your tarot practice. Make sure you're stretching and challenging yourself with more difficult daily readings. The point is for you to struggle at first, and even to get things wrong, because that's how you learn.

One reason why some people struggle with a daily draw is that it's so open-ended. There are a lot of potential answers to "What's going to happen today?" and when you're new to tarot, that can be overwhelming. The best way around this, I find, is to ask a more specific question. Each day, ask about a particular event or interaction that you're expecting. "How will my 2:30 meeting go?" or "Will I have a good time on my date?" is a much more specific, more manageable question. Doing more pointed readings is easier, less intimidating, and just as rewarding as doing a general daily draw.

The most important thing about learning tarot is to practice all the time. Find something to read tarot about every single day, even if it's just "Should I order pizza for dinner?" There will certainly be days when you don't feel like reading or can't think of a question to ask. Read anyway. Doing a daily draw is like running the scales when you practice piano; you are drilling the fundamental skills of tarot into your brain so that you don't have to consciously think about them when you start to take on more challenging work. As we continue on in this book, we will start to look at more advanced, complex interpretive techniques, but all of tarot reading relies on the essential skills that you will develop with the practice of a daily draw.

How Does Tarot Work?

Ask three tarot readers how tarot works and you're liable to get five different answers. There is no consensus, no official explanation, as to the underlying mechanism of tarot. Many readers will simply shrug their shoulders and say something to the effect of, "I don't know why it works, and I don't particularly care. All that matters is that it *does* work." Nonetheless, it's worth taking a minute to think about the question of why, because our understanding of what tarot is can influence how we use it.

There are a variety of potential explanations for how a tarot reading works, ranging from the mundane and psychological to the downright magical. You can subscribe to any of these explanations and be an excellent tarot reader, but readers with different views of what tarot is will (understandably) have different approaches to using it.

Commonalities across Tarot Practices

Tarot is such a diverse practice that no aspect of tarot reading (excepting the simple fact of using a tarot deck) can truly be called universal. However, there are a few general points of common agreement. These views about tarot are widespread and broadly uncontroversial.

Tarot Relies on Randomness

This much is evident: if you're going to read tarot, you need to shuffle your cards thoroughly. Tarot works by drawing cards at random; you don't know in advance which card you're going to draw. In order for that to be effective, your deck has to be properly randomized, which means it has to be well shuffled. The last thing you want is to do a reading for someone and draw all the same cards that you had in your previous reading simply because you didn't mix the deck enough!

The way you shuffle your deck is entirely a matter of personal preference. I grew up in Nevada, the land of casinos, so I opt for a riffle-and-bridge shuffle. Other readers opt for an overhand shuffle or even a game of seventy-eight-card pickup. Whatever works for you is fine as long as you mix the cards thoroughly. Likewise, people have different approaches to drawing cards out of the deck. When I'm performing a reading, I will cut the deck and then draw all my cards off the top (once again, very Vegas). I know other readers who fan the deck out and pull each card from a different spot, letting their intuition guide them.

Open Questions Work Best

If you only take away one thing from this book, let it be this: *tarot is storytelling*. It works through symbolism and narrative. Each card has images printed on it that symbolize various ideas, from the big and cosmic (e.g., fate and agency) to the human and mundane (e.g., grief and nostalgia). The interpretation of a tarot reading is all about linking these themes together, both with each other and with the question that has been asked, in order to tell a story.

This means that tarot works best with open-ended questions—the sort of question where you have room to tell a story properly. With methods of divination, it's tempting to ask closed questions, the sort that can be answered with a simple yes or no, but those questions are less than ideal for tarot as a medium. Tarot excels when it has room for nuance, complexity, and depth, and a plain old "Does he love me?" often doesn't allow for those things.

That said, closed questions aren't always a bad thing. Oftentimes, a closed question can lead you to an open one. You may ask "Does he love me?" and find yourself answering that question in a roundabout way when your cards provide a broader description of your lover's feelings for you and the direction your relationship is headed. The most important thing is that you allow yourself to be open to all the information that comes through in a reading. Embrace the story that your cards are trying to tell. It's okay to ask a yes or no question so long as you leave room for the answer to be bigger than the question you asked.

Consider the following questions. All the ones on the left are closed; the ones on the right are ways to rephrase the same ideas in order to allow more breathing room. Remember, it's not that tarot *can't* answer the sort of question on the left. It's just that tarot lends itself to the complexity of the questions on the right, and if you ask the former question, you may often find yourself answering the latter anyway. Tarot encourages us to look at the bigger picture.

Closed	Open
Does he love me?	How does he feel about me?
Will I get the job?	What's going to happen in my career?
Should I move to Albuquerque?	Where will I be happiest?
Did my interview go well?	When can I expect to hear back?
Is this project dead in the water?	Who can help me revitalize this project?
Should I forgive my sister after our fight?	Why did I get so angry with my sister?

You may notice a common thread among the questions in the right-hand column. They're all open questions, starting with the basic words *who, what, when, where, why,* and *how.* Each of these questions requires more than a one-word answer. They have different sorts of subject matter, ranging from love to career to family life. Some of them are about decision-making, some of them are predictive questions about the future, some are introspective, and some are simply asking for clarity about what's happening. Nonetheless, these are all questions that are answered by telling a story. That's the ideal way to approach tarot.

Tarot Can Rely on Intuition, Analysis, or Both

There are two basic components to any tarot reading: the left brain and the right brain. The left brain is the intellectual, analytic side. In tarot, that's the part that memorizes card meanings, learns various layouts, and studies the elemental correspondences of the cards. The right brain, on the other hand, is the intuitive, artistic side. In tarot, this is the part of reading that doesn't come out of a book, but instead comes from your own gut feelings and intuition.

You use both parts of yourself in a tarot reading. You need the left brain and the right brain, thinking and feeling. Different readers will combine these skills in different measures. Some readers are very formal and analytic, looking at all kinds of astrological and elemental correspondences for each card, taking detailed notes about the whole deck, and trying only to read with the "official" meanings of the seventy-eight tarot cards. Other readers swing in the opposite direction, eschewing the interpretations given in books and focusing instead on their own interpretation of card imagery and their intuitive feelings about what a card means in a given context.

Striking the balance and learning how much to think and how much to feel takes time, practice, and a certain amount of self-knowledge. We'll talk in part III about more intuitive approaches to tarot reading, but throughout this book, remember: what you feel is just as important as what I (or any other tarot author) might say. It's okay—and encouraged—for you to have your own insights and ideas as you develop your relationship with the cards, and for those ideas to differ from what you read in books. Likewise, if you're feeling stuck and having a hard time interpreting something, it's always okay to fall back on established tarot tradition. Don't be afraid to look up the meanings of the cards or to use memorized keywords, even as you gain more experience.

Differing Perspectives

Everyone has their own views about these matters, and there is no authority to say who's right and who's wrong, so the purpose of this survey is not to convince you of any one view. Rather, it's to help you orient yourself and see how other people think about tarot in order to figure out your own views. Some of these explanations of tarot will likely be more palatable to you than others. It's possible that you may find multiple explanations plausible, or that you may come to have your own ideas that don't align with any of the positions noted here. That's okay. The goal is for you to reach an understanding of tarot that feels right to you; it doesn't have to match up with what anyone else says.

Tarot Awakens Your Latent Psychic Abilities

Perhaps the most commonly held view about tarot is that the real psychism isn't in the cards—it's in us, the readers. In this view, every person has innate psychic abilities that can be brought out through training and practice. Tarot cards are a way of helping to unlock the psychic abilities you already have. The cards give you something to focus on, a starting point to help you direct your psychic energy. They're like a psychic radio, picking up on ambient signals and translating them into meaningful messages that your ordinary mind is able to perceive.

People who think about tarot this way tend to think that there's nothing special about the cards, per se. Tarot is, simply put, a tool that helps you pick up on your own psychic gifts. A reader might use a deck of tarot cards, but they also might accomplish the same effect with a scrying mirror, a set of runes, dream interpretation, or some other method.

Readers who subscribe to this view tend to heavily emphasize the need for intuition in readings. Because the point of tarot cards is to facilitate your own psychic abilities, the argument goes, an important part of reading is learning how to trust yourself when a message pops up. If you pull the Three of Cups and something about it tells you that your querent is going to receive good news from her sister—even if you can't rationalize *why* you get that impression—that message is likely exactly what your psychic mind is trying to communicate. Part of accessing your innate psychism is learning to trust yourself when you have a strong gut feeling that the cards are saying something particular but you can't explain exactly why.

Tarot Accesses Your Subconscious Mind

A similar—but slightly less magical—view is that tarot allows us to communicate with our own subconscious minds. This view understands the subconscious as the part of ourselves that, by definition, is not accessible through ordinary thought and communication. It's all of our repressed desires, fears, memories, motivations, and so on. We can't just sit down and have a conversation with the subconscious mind, because conversation is something conscious. The subconscious responds not to ideas and words, but to symbolism, imagery, and emotion. Therefore, we can reach out to the subconscious and understand ourselves better through the symbol-laden medium of tarot.

Readers who take this more psychological perspective will tend to prefer tarot for introspective questions. Rather than asking "What's going to happen?" they will ask things like "What's really motivating me in this situation?" or "What am I not seeing?" This is an approach to tarot that tends to prioritize individual agency and the importance of self-awareness in informing our choices.

Tarot Relies on Synchronicity

Synchronicity is an oft-misunderstood term coined by the Swiss psychoanalyst Carl Jung. In his book *Synchronicity: An Acausal Connecting Principle*, Jung describes synchronicity as a meaningful coincidence: a set of overlapping events that are not causally connected to each other, but that nonetheless hold some meaning or relevance to what's going on in our lives.[1] For example, suppose that you're talking to a friend about wanting to go back to school and finish your college degree. Immediately after that conversation, you head to your local coffee shop, and on your way there, you're cut off by a car with a bumper sticker for the local state university. In line at the coffee shop, you're standing behind someone wearing a sweatshirt from the same school, and on your way out the door, you notice a flyer for the school, which wasn't there the last time you got coffee.

All of these events, independently of each other, have no particular meaning. Moreover, there's no causal connection between them. None of them caused any of the others to happen, and it's pure coincidence that you had so many college-related experiences all in a row. Nevertheless, these events are meaningful. Even if it's only by chance that you saw that bumper sticker, sweatshirt, and flyer, those things are all relevant to the conversation you were having with your friend and your decision about whether or not to go

---

1. C. G. Jung, *Synchronicity: An Acausal Connecting Principle*, trans. R. F. C. Hull (Princeton, NJ: Princeton University Press, 1973), 10.

back to school. Those were the right things for you to see at that time in order to convince you that finishing your degree is the right choice to make. These events, though totally unrelated to each other by any causal mechanism, all came together in the exact right way to give you a sign. They formed a series of meaningful coincidences—that is to say, a synchronicity.

Many tarot readers see the process of tarot reading as creating the opportunity for synchronicities so that people can receive meaningful or important messages. We draw the cards at random, but we trust that there will be some meaningful connection between the cards we pull and the question we have asked. There's no particular explanation as to why the "right" cards come up for a reading; from this view, it's pure coincidence. It is, however, a meaningful coincidence. When you ask a question and pull a tarot card, you trust that the card you choose will have a message for you and will be synchronistically relevant to the subject at hand. Even if you can't explain why you pulled *this* card and not *that* one, you still find significance in the card you drew, and you interpret it with the understanding that—through some mysterious mechanism—it contains the answer to your question.

Tarot Is Apophenia

Apophenia is the process by which humans perceive meaningful patterns in random information. It's what happens when we look at the stars and make constellations out of them, when we go cloud-gazing, or when we see Elvis Presley's face on a piece of burnt toast. It's also how we ascribe causal connection to coincidences and unrelated events. We see examples of this all the time: when someone says that "bad news comes in threes," when a gambler claims to be on a hot streak, or when someone glances at the clock at precisely 11:11 and finds meaning in the number. It is an essential feature of humanity that we perceive patterns in the world around us and that we ascribe meaning to those patterns. Some people think that tarot works in largely the same way.

This is a particularly skeptical outlook on tarot reading. According to this view, there's nothing supernatural or psychic going on with tarot at all. Readers who take this view argue that it's not important which cards actually turn up in a reading; what matters is the process of interpretation, where we ascribe meaning to the cards by filling in information and making the reading relevant to our situation. From this view, it doesn't matter whether you pull the Seven of Pentacles or the Three of Swords; either way, you will be able to see some connection between that card and the situation you're asking about—simply because seeing connections is what humans inexorably do. Tarot provides you with the framework to conduct this meaning-making process. It gives you a place to look for significant patterns so that you can fill those patterns out with the details of your own life and reflect on your various questions and problems.

Tarot Works through the Assistance of Tutelary Spirits

Some tarot readers believe that tarot works because of the intercession of spirits of one kind of another: angel guides, ancestors, or even a deity or deities. Readers who take this perspective often also have experience as psychic mediums and work with spirits in some other way. They view tarot as an avenue of communication between themselves and spirits who have access to more information than them, and who are therefore better equipped to answer questions. Such tarot readers will often preface a reading with a short prayer or petition, addressing their tutelary spirits and asking for help.

Practice Reading: How Tarot Works

What better way to consider how tarot works than to ask your tarot deck? Begin by thinking about your perspective on tarot for a while. How do you think it works? What are your general thoughts? You don't have to have a fully developed theory; your rough thoughts on the matter are more than sufficient. Make note of these thoughts in your tarot journal. Then, shuffle the cards and ask "How does tarot work?" Pull one card and interpret it according to the process outlined in the previous practice readings.

Is the message of this card in line with the ideas you had already jotted down? Or is it something different and challenging to your preexisting worldview? How does it encourage you to frame (or reframe) your perspective on tarot? Write all of this down in your tarot journal. That way, if your perspective changes over time, you'll be able to come back to this entry and see how your ideas have grown.

It's What Works for You

Ultimately, what matters most in tarot is what makes sense to you as an individual reader. The perspectives provided in this book are here to help you get a sense of the possibilities with tarot and of the different ways that you could approach it, think about it, and use it. Don't hesitate to experiment. Try using tarot for things you wouldn't normally use it for, just to see how it feels. If you're generally inclined to see tarot as an expression of your own subconscious, step outside of your comfort zone and do a predictive reading about what's going to happen in your life tomorrow. If you view tarot as working through angel guides, do a reading or two without asking your guides for assistance, just to see what happens.

As a novice, you are not expected to have all of the answers as to how tarot works. Quite the contrary, in fact. This is a time for you to explore tarot, to figure out what works for you and what doesn't, and to learn what you like and dislike. Don't be in a rush to form crystallized opinions. Instead, try a little bit of everything, and be open to the experiences that come your way.

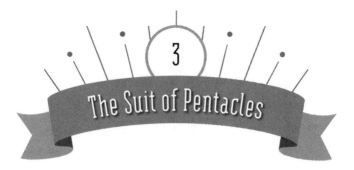

The Suit of Pentacles

This is the first of our chapters detailing the interpretations of the seventy-eight cards in a tarot deck. In this chapter, we'll focus on the suit of Pentacles from the Minor Arcana. This suit corresponds to the element of earth, and all the cards in it deal with themes of money, possessions, health, work, and material circumstances. In this chapter, we'll only be looking at the numbered cards in the suit (that is to say, the Ace through Ten); the court cards are discussed in chapter 15.

Ace of Pentacles

Aces in tarot represent new beginnings, and the Ace of Pentacles is specifically the beginning of something material. It could be a new job, a new house, an investment opportunity, a sudden windfall, news about your health, or anything similar that introduces a new thing into your immediate, physical, practical life.

The image on this card classically depicts a hand holding a pentacle in a lush garden; implicit here is the symbolism of planting a seed. The Ace of Pentacles contains the potential for future growth. It gives you the germ of something that, if you put time and care into it, can grow and bloom. What we see in the Ace of Pentacles is the very beginning of *something* before it's certain what exactly that something will become; it is the planting, the sowing. The

Ace of Pentacles appears in a reading when you're doing the preparatory work for something and making room in your life for new growth, but you don't know what exactly the fruits of your labor will be. You are planting a seed of possibility, and you don't yet know what that seed will grow into.

Importantly, not every seed grows into what we hope it to be. The Ace of Pentacles does not promise, nor guarantee, success in the new venture it signals. Sometimes we start something and it looks promising to begin with, but as time goes on we lose enthusiasm, stop working at it, and don't see the payoff we had initially expected. The Ace of Pentacles is only a beginning; it says nothing about how things will end. When this card shows up in a reading, it tells us that now is a time for us to plant a seed—but there is still a great deal of work to be done after the seed is planted. It must be watered, nurtured, and attended to, and the burden is on us to do the necessary work that allows the potential of the Ace to blossom into actuality.

More than any other card in the deck, the Ace of Pentacles reminds us that starting a new project takes work. Success rarely falls into your lap. Most of the time, you have to go out and make it happen. This card points to a need for action; an opportunity has come your way, and it's your responsibility to seize that opportunity and make the most of it. Pick up the phone and make a call, put together a business proposal, or pick up a hammer and start building. The Ace of Pentacles has potential for greatness, but only if you do something about it.

Not all beginnings are good—or easy. Sometimes the Ace of Pentacles signals difficulties or obstructions with getting a project off the ground, or it can point to the arrival of unwelcome news about earthy subjects like money, work, or health. In any case, this card is what we make of it. Even hardship and frustration can be dealt with, and the Ace of Pentacles shows us that something is coming over the horizon that demands our action, one way or another.

Two of Pentacles

The Two of Pentacles is a balancing act. This card classically depicts a juggler tossing two pentacles, and the message is invariably about the need for balance, consideration, and restraint. Because the suit of Pentacles deals with material considerations, the most literal interpretation of this card is the need for someone to look at their finances and balance their budget. However, in a broader sense, the Two of Pentacles can speak to any situation where someone needs to get their life under control and begin to manage the disparate and chaotic forces affecting them. The Two of Pentacles cries out for balance and equity of all kinds: in finances, interpersonal relationships, work/life balance, and so on.

The central theme of this card is balance, which is most needed at the times when our lives are truly imbalanced. The Two of Pentacles often shows up in readings when someone is in over their head and doesn't know what they're doing or when they're overwhelmed with obligations and don't know how to manage everything. This is the card that tells us to take a deep breath and trust that we can figure everything out, but our problems won't solve themselves magically. We have to look at our lives with an unflinching eye and evaluate how much we're trying to do and how realistic our commitments actually are. Balance can be achieved, but it requires hard work, diligence, and—sometimes—unpleasant sacrifices. Whether it's a matter of curbing your spending or turning down offers for things you would like to do but simply don't have the time for, the Two of Pentacles carries a gentle reminder that in order to find balance, sometimes you have to offload excess weight.

The message of this card is not always so grim, though. Watching a juggler who is off-balance is a painful sight, but when a juggler knows what they're doing and is in control, they become graceful, effortless, and fluid. When our lives are in balance, everything just works. The Two of Pentacles tells us to strive for the kind of balance that feels easy so that we don't feel overwhelmed by the things we're trying to do. Like the master juggler, we want to be able to move without thought and without worry, keeping all our balls in the air as easily as we breathe. That's something we accomplish by knowing our own strengths and weaknesses, working to develop our skills where needed, and choosing not to take on more than we can handle.

Balance is something achieved reciprocally. There is an innate ebb and flow to it, a give and take. If we start doing something new, we sacrifice something else in order to have time for it. If we get better at something and learn how to do it more easily, we can take on more challenging work. This can feel onerous at times, but it doesn't have to be. Through the Two of Pentacles, the constant juggle of keeping balance in our lives can become a joyful dance.

Three of Pentacles

The Three of Pentacles is a card of teamwork and dynamism. Where the Two taught us moderation and balance, the Three encourages us to grow and test our limits. This card depicts an architect consulting with a couple about the construction of an archway. It's a card of cooperation, of exchanging ideas with other people and learning from them in order to make our work better. The architect in this image is the expert. He is a master of his craft, and he has the confidence to do what he does and do it well. Nonetheless, he chooses to coordinate with the other figures in the card, soliciting their input on his project. He knows that as good as he is, he is made stronger by the help of others.

It can be difficult for us to work with others, to ask for their ideas and to take those ideas seriously—sometimes at the expense of realizing our own. Nonetheless, the Three of Pentacles reminds us that other people have strengths we don't have. They can see things we don't see and come up with ideas we'd never have considered. Working with other people can be a humbling experience. So often we have a vision in our minds of how we want our work to turn out, and we don't want to surrender that vision to the influence of other people. It can feel like abdicating our autonomy. But cooperation is not subjugation. When we work dynamically with other people, we don't give up our own vision; we merely add other perspectives. If we can bring ourselves to accept the help of others, and to work as part of a team rather than trying to go it alone, the result of our labor will be that much the better.

Sometimes, teamwork grinds to a halt. People have difficulty communicating and working well together, egos get in the way, and we can lose sight of the bigger picture. In circumstances like these, the Three of Pentacles appears as a nudge in the direction of humility and cooperation. All the cards in the suit of Pentacles demand work of us, and the Three demands the work of being with other people, which can sometimes be the most difficult task of all. This card reminds us that we cannot, in fact, do everything on our own, and that other people are there to lift us up rather than drag us down. It also reminds us that we have a reciprocal duty to lift others up and to help them in their goals just as they help us in ours. More than anything else, this card tells us that our strengths are to be found in our connection to other people and in fostering partnerships that are mutually supportive, encouraging, and beneficial. Humans are social animals. We're at our best when we're together.

Four of Pentacles

Not every card in the tarot is inspiring and uplifting. Some of them force us to reflect on our negative traits, our unhealthy patterns of behavior, or the bad things that come our way. In the suit of Pentacles, which deals with the material side of life, it is unsurprising, then, that we have a card to embody themes of selfishness, materialism, and covetousness. This card is the Four of Pentacles.

The Four of Pentacles depicts a man sitting possessively atop a pile of coins, clutching one of them to his chest. This is a card that says *mine*—my money, my home, my friends, my everything. It's about latching on to something, laying claim to it as your own, and refusing to let go. In the most literal sense, the Four of Pentacles can represent a miser, someone selfish and greedy who is unwilling to expend time or money for the betterment of others. However, it need not only be monetary. In a broader sense, the Four of Pentacles is about the feeling of being closed off, shutting out the rest of the world and deciding to care only about yourself.

This attitude is not inherently a bad thing, and there are times where it's called for. The Four of Pentacles represents a concern with one's own basic security and well-being, and in times of scarcity, when you don't know how you're going to afford your next meal, this is an understandable and even appropriate reaction. The Four of Pentacles is someone who saves for a rainy day, who builds up a nest egg, who keeps money under their mattress just in case something disastrous happens. However, when taken too far, this impulse can turn into selfishness, greed, and even a willful disregard for the needs of others—the attitude that makes people say, "I'm only looking out for number one."

The Four of Pentacles craves security but often mistakes openness for instability. It aims to close itself off, building walls around itself so that threats can't get in and resources can't slip out, but it does so at peril of isolating itself from everything that makes life worth living. This card challenges us to let go of the things we cling to in order to make room for actually living our lives. This could mean letting go of penny-pinching, but it can also be entrenched ideas, coping mechanisms, and patterns of behavior that no longer serve us. It's natural to want to hold on to things that feel familiar and safe, but if we hold too tightly, we get stuck where we are. With the Four of Pentacles, we learn that it's okay to seek stability and comfort, but it's also okay to let go and allow a bit of uncertainty into our lives.

Five of Pentacles

The Five of Pentacles is another difficult card. It depicts two ailing figures (one of whom is on crutches) standing outside a church window in the middle of a blizzard. Fives in tarot are cards of hardship and strife, and the Five of Pentacles is the very real hardship that can affect our material lives. The Four of Pentacles worried about insecurity, and the Five sees those worries actualized: poverty, illness, bad luck, and destitution. The Five of Pentacles shows up in readings when someone is having a hard time and going through a bad period in their life, potentially through no fault of their own.

The message of the Five of Pentacles is one that we all know deep down, although it's something we don't like to hear. Sometimes life sucks. The world isn't fair, and bad things can happen to us whether we deserve them or not. Learning how to cope with those bad things is an inescapable part of life.

Although this is a bleak card, it is far from hopeless. Remember, the Minor Arcana are the "lesser mysteries" of the tarot; they represent ordinary, everyday concerns. The Five of Pentacles presents us with troubles, yes, but only because that's what life is like. We have bad days, and sometimes bad days can turn into bad weeks or bad months. It can feel like the universe is conspiring against us, but the Five of Pentacles suggests that this isn't the case. Sometimes our hardship is mundane and ordinary, and when those times come, the only thing we can do is keep our chin up and try to survive until the next good day. The Five of Pentacles teaches us that the world is a tough place and sometimes life can be cruel, but when that happens, the only thing to do is get through it.

The figures in this card are sick, poor, and out alone in the cold. Things look hopeless for them. Even so, they know that if they can just make it through the night and weather this storm, the sun will rise and tomorrow might be a little bit better. There's no guarantee of that, and the next day might be just as bad as the day before, but they can hold out hope. Likewise, when the Five of Pentacles shows up in a reading, it's unflinching in its message. Things are going to get hard, or maybe they already have. Even so, hardship can be weathered.

The Five of Pentacles does not carry with it a guarantee that everything will be okay in the end, because sometimes things don't end up okay. What it does carry, though, is the message that you are not helpless. Even when you feel powerless, even when everything in your life has gone wrong, simply surviving counts as a victory. Find a place to hunker down and wait for the storm to pass. Sometimes that is enough.

Six of Pentacles

In the Six of Pentacles, we see a lesson learned from the Four and Five. The Four was selfish and closed off for fear of loss, and the Five actually experienced that loss. The Six shows maturity and growth as a result of the hardships we have undergone. In this card, we learn to do what the Four of Pentacles could not: Namely, think beyond ourselves and care for other people. The Six of Pentacles is a card of charity, kindness, and compassion. It's about helping those who are less fortunate than us—or, conversely, about receiving help from those who are in a position to give it.

This card shows a figure holding a pair of scales and handing out coins to beggars on the street. Fundamentally, it is about kindness. Not kindness as an emotional state, as something internal that we experience for our own benefit, but rather the kindness that we *do*, the way we demonstrate concern for others by going out into the world and taking care of them. When the Six of Pentacles sees a disaster relief telethon, it doesn't just say, "Oh, how terrible." It sits down and writes a check.

As with all the cards in this suit, the Six of Pentacles has a wider range of meanings beyond monetary exchange. It can mean volunteering your time, offering emotional support and guidance to people who are vulnerable, or being someone who helps fix other people's problems. In the most general sense, this card is about equity and redistribution, and about resetting relationships that are imbalanced. One person has more than another, needs something that someone else is able to give, or has authority or expertise that establishes a power dynamic. There is an inequality of one sort or another. The Six of Pentacles transforms that inequality when the person with more gives to the person with less. It is about the flow from one person to another, not as a bargain or a contract, but as an act of kindness freely given.

Note that not all forms of inequality are bad. The relationship between a mentor and a student is an unequal one; the mentor has knowledge and experience that the student lacks. The Six of Pentacles nevertheless shows that relationship becoming more equal over time, as the mentor shares their expertise and the student becomes knowledgeable in their own right. This card encompasses all forms of giving, sharing, and improving the lives of others. When we see the Six of Pentacles in a reading, we may be on either end, giving or receiving. Learning how to receive compassion and charity can be even harder than learning how to give it. This card teaches us to help others when they need it, but also to accept charity when it is offered.

Seven of Pentacles

In the Seven of Pentacles, we see a gardener working on his crops. He's far past the planting stage, and his work is beginning to look like it'll bear fruit—golden coins have begun to sprout from the vine—but there's still a long way to go before his work pays off. The Seven of Pentacles is a card of waiting, a card that cautions us against rashness and impatience. When we get antsy because we feel we've worked hard enough and we want our reward *now*, the Seven of Pentacles shushes us and tells us, "Not now, but soon enough."

Pluck a fruit from the vine before it's ready, and it will be bitter and under-ripe. Set a pot on the stove and sit in front of it to watch, and it feels like it takes forever to boil. Open your oven too frequently to check on the progress of a cake, and you might ruin the whole thing. When we allow impatience to overtake our actions, we risk spoiling the things we anticipate. The message of the Seven of Pentacles is that the things we're waiting for aren't quite ready yet, and we need to wait a little bit longer if we want them to turn out right. Waiting can be agony, but the Seven of Pentacles promises that patience is the best course of action. Whatever we desire, the time is not yet right for us to get it.

Patience does not equal passivity, however. The gardener in this card isn't ready to harvest his fruit yet, but that doesn't mean there is no work for him to do. On the contrary, he has a great deal of work: weeding, watering, and caring for his plant so that it can grow properly. The Seven of Pentacles tells us that it's too early to try to harvest; it does *not* tell us that we should sit around twiddling our thumbs. Indeed, we have more work to do if we want a successful harvest to come. This card, then, is about staying in the moment and doing the hard work that needs to be done, rather than fantasizing about skipping ahead to the payoff.

All of the cards in the suit of Pentacles ground us in reality, in the immediate here and now. The Seven of Pentacles, especially, tells us to keep our heads down and focus on what needs to be done in the present moment, rather than getting distracted by fantasies about the future. This card doesn't care about what you're going to do someday—it cares about what needs to get done now. Concentrate on the work, not the reward, because you need to do the former before the latter can be a possibility.

Eight of Pentacles

Like the Seven, the Eight of Pentacles teaches us to invest ourselves in work, but it is work of a different kind. Here, we see an apprentice craftsman practicing his trade. This card deals with study, practice, and the sort of work it takes to acquire new skills and knowledge. It is most often associated with students and schools, but it can also mean practicing a new skill (like a musical instrument), being guided by a mentor or supervisor, vocational training, continuing education, or any other form of training or study. The point of the Eight of Pentacles is that everything we learn—from calculus to changing a tire—requires work.

The experience of being a novice at something can be challenging and humbling. Most of us don't enjoy feeling like we're not good at something. Unfortunately, when we first start trying to learn something new, we will inevitably not be very good at it. That's how learning goes; you make mistakes over and over again, and slowly you build up experience and expertise by learning from the mistakes you have made. If you take a pottery class, your first attempt at throwing clay will come out lopsided and wobbly, as will your second and your third. But if you stick with it and put in the time, you can gradually become more confident and consistent in your work. The Eight of Pentacles is the card of putting in that time.

When the Eight of Pentacles appears in a reading, it tells us to be comfortable with the process of learning. We don't have all the skills or all the knowledge we want, but that's okay. Gaining those skills is a process. The Eight of Pentacles encourages us to accept the things we don't know so that we can devote the time and energy to learning them properly. It can be tempting to puff out our chests and pretend we already know everything, but in the long run, doing so will serve no purpose. Posturing and bluffing won't make us experts. The only road to genuine expertise involves diligent study and practice.

It is also important to remember that we are not alone when we try to learn new things. We are able to seek help from people who know more than we do, and in fact we are encouraged to do so. The apprentice depicted in the Eight of Pentacles studies under a master craftsman who can oversee his work, show him proper technique, and critique him when he errs. An important component of the Eight of Pentacles is the idea that when you're trying to learn something new, you should draw on all the resources available to you, and that other people count among those resources. Once again, it can be humbling to ask for instruction, and it might chafe at your pride. Nevertheless, the best way to learn is to be taught by someone who knows what they're doing.

Nine of Pentacles

The Nine of Pentacles is the card where we finally see the rewards of our labor. All throughout the suit of Pentacles, we have seen cards that encouraged us to work, to wait, to budget and balance and plan. Here in the Nine, we see what all that work was for. An extravagantly dressed woman walks through a lush garden with a songbird perched on her finger. This is a woman who has achieved everything she strived for and is now living in the lap of luxury. The Nine of Pentacles is the card where we get what we've been working for.

This is not just a card of good things falling out of the sky for no reason. We only get to this point after we have worked our way through the rest of the suit of Pentacles, after we have rolled up our sleeves and done the work that was required of us. The imagery of a garden pervades the suit of

Pentacles, and we can understand that it is the same garden throughout. The seed we planted in the Ace of Pentacles and the ground we tilled in the Seven are the same as in the Nine. The flourishing we see here is the direct result of the work we put in earlier. The Nine of Pentacles is only abundant because we have made it so.

The Nine of Pentacles tells us that we get out of a project what we put into it. Of course, this means that if we have neglected our work, we can't expect the payoff. If we've been dishonest and underhanded with our colleagues and clients—if we've cheated and swindled and lied—we may well be repaid in kind. When the Nine of Pentacles appears in a reading, it is time for us to get what's coming to us and to experience the consequences of our actions. If we've been diligent about our work, those consequences will be positive, but if we haven't, we can't expect money to rain down from the sky. This is a card that rewards us for what we've done, but in order to get that reward, we have to have actually done something for it.

The successful, flourishing, abundant energy of the Nine of Pentacles can also manifest as public recognition for a job well done. Winning a trophy, earning a commendation, receiving a certificate or degree—all of these are moments when we are acknowledged by others for our excellence, when we are seen for the work we've done. Recognition, reward, and hard-earned success are the key themes of this card. The Nine of Pentacles tells us to appreciate our beautiful gardens and to enjoy finally getting the things we've spent so much time working toward. The time for work is past; now it's time for enjoyment, leisure, and celebration.

Ten of Pentacles

At long last, we have completed our journey through the Suit of Pentacles. The Ten of each suit is the card where the suit's themes come together—where everything is wrapped up with a neat little bow. In the material, practical suit of Pentacles, this means a consideration of the ways we shape—and are shaped by—our material conditions. The Ten of Pentacles depicts a family sitting in front of a large estate. The building is the same one we saw under construction in the Three, and in the background, we can just catch a glimpse of the estate's verdant garden. The family itself comprises three generations: a grandparent, a set of parents, and a young child.

This is a card about inheritances, legacies, and descent. It's about the things we get from our ancestors, our families, and our material circumstances more broadly. The Ten of Pentacles shows us everything that is passed down through the generations, everything that comes to us as a result not only of our own labor, but of the labor of those who have gone before. This can range from literal financial endowments to cultural inheritances like language or cuisine. The Ten of Pentacles can be a gift, a donation, or just a lesson learned from someone who is older and wiser.

This card is fundamentally about your history and how your history shapes who you are. History includes your own past, but is not limited to it; the Ten of Pentacles encompasses the history of everyone who shapes your life. This card is particularly relevant to your relationship with your elders, family members, and authority figures like teachers or bosses. When the Ten of Pentacles appears in a reading, it directs your attention to the question of how your life has been affected by outside influences. No person is an island; you are inexorably connected to people and events that came before you. To understand yourself, you first have to understand their impact on you. To know your place in the world, you have to know where you stand relative to others. What have you inherited from your predecessors? How is your world different because of them?

A complementary understanding of this card is that you also leave a legacy for those who come after you. Just as your world is different because of your lineage, so too will the people who follow find that you have changed the world for them. The Ten of Pentacles invites you to be conscious, not just of the inheritance you've received, but also of the one you will pass on. How do you leave things different than you found them? How do you make the world a better place for the people who are going to inhabit it after you are gone? The Ten of Pentacles turns our eye to the past and the future. We must understand the interconnection of past, present, and future so that we appreciate the full weight of the things we do in the present moment.

PART II

INTELLECTUAL

4

Spreads and Card Layouts

Tarot is storytelling. Most stories, however, can't be told with just one idea. Stories are complex narratives with multiple characters, events, and themes. At the very least, they have a beginning, a middle, and an end. In order to tell stories right, we want to capture all of their nuance. Likewise, in order to read tarot right, we often need more than one card in a reading. Simple questions can be answered with just one card, but if we want a bigger picture, we'll need to introduce multiple cards in order to capture the nuance of the various forces at work.

A multi-card layout used for a tarot reading is known as a *spread*. Tarot spreads can be large or small, simple or complex, or ranging from two cards to (in some cases) the full seventy-eight-card deck. In many spreads, each card position has a specific meaning; you identify the major points of information that you need to answer your question, pull one card for each of those points, and analyze each card individually. In this way, you break a complex answer to your reading down into smaller, more manageable components. Then, once you've looked at each card individually, you can put them together to see how they work as a cohesive whole.

Figuring out which spread is appropriate for a given question is an acquired skill. Additional cards can give more nuance to a reading, which is quite useful, but if you have too many cards in a spread, the glut of information can make it difficult to sort out what's relevant and what's not. As a general rule, three-card spreads are sufficient for many questions, and the most complex and tangled issues might require as many as twelve. I'd encourage you not to overuse spreads with more than a dozen cards, at least while you're in the early stages of learning tarot; the goal is not to overwhelm yourself, but to add just enough information to be useful in your reading.

Three-Card Past/Present/Future Spread

One of the simplest and most effective tarot spreads is only three cards: one for the past, one for the present, and one for the future. This gives us a narrative arc for our readings, a beginning-middle-end progression. It allows us to show not only where we are right now, but also where we've been, where we're going, and how those things are connected.

To use this spread, shuffle your cards and ask your question. Then, pull three cards and arrange them in a horizontal line, with the first card on the far left and the third card on the far right:

Past/Present/Future Spread

To interpret a spread, begin with the same process that you've used for your one-card readings. Start with the first card in the spread. Identify the imagery, the major symbols, and the overall impression it gives you. Then, look up the description of the card in this book and think about how it complements what you got from your intuition. Bring those two things together and try to synthesize them in one or two sentences. The only difference is that rather than providing an answer to the reading as a whole, you're answering only part of the question: the part represented by that card's position in the spread. If you draw the Five of Pentacles in the "past" position, for example, you would say that someone has recently come out of a period of serious hardship; if you draw the same card in the "future" position, you would say that things might be okay right now, but it looks like they're going to get rocky soon.

In this way, you can get more information out of a reading with multiple cards than you could with just one. Of course, reading with multiple cards is more than just doing a series of one-card readings; you also want to think about how the cards connect to each other and form a coherent story. We'll have the opportunity to explore these narrative-building techniques in depth in subsequent chapters, but the basic principle is this. How do the themes from the cards you've drawn relate to each other? Are they similar? Are they different? Is there a noticeable progression? Is there a problem or tension between some of the cards? You'll get a better feel for how to identify these connections as you practice more, but it's a good idea to start looking for them now.

Practice Reading: A Career Change

Let's do a reading together. Suppose a woman comes to you for a reading. She tells you that she runs a successful accounting firm, but lately she has been considering changing her career path and becoming a professional chef. She wants to know what the best course of action is. You shuffle your deck and draw three cards: the Nine of Pentacles, the Four of Cups, and the Eight of Pentacles.

1	2	3
Nine of Pentacles	*Four of Cups*	*Eight of Pentacles*

The Nine of Pentacles in the "past" position confirms what she's already told you. She has built a solid, lucrative business and has spent many years enjoying the success she's earned for herself. However, when you look at the Four of Cups in the "present" position, you notice that the figure looks dissatisfied. You look up the Four of Cups in this book, and you see that this card deals with themes of stagnation, disaffection, and being in a rut. This tells you that although things were great in the past, they are no longer. Your querent is unhappy with her life as it is, and something needs to change.

Finally, looking at the "future" card, you see the Eight of Pentacles: work, study, and learning. Yes, something needs to change in your querent's life, but she doesn't currently have the skills to start her life over. She might want to become a chef, but she's not trained as one. The Eight of Pentacles suggests that the next thing she needs to do, the way to move her life forward, is to go back to school and receive vocational training in her new field. At present, she doesn't have what it would take to open her own restaurant, but if she puts in the effort to acquire those skills, the road is open for her.

Reading with a spread is a dynamic process. You want to look at what each card is doing individually, but the information you get from one card affects what you may find in the others. In this case, the Four of Cups in the center drives you forward and tells you that yes, this woman really does need to make a change in her life; the Eight of Pentacles then specifies what that change should be. If you'd drawn a different card in the "present" position, the interpretation of the Eight of Pentacles might have been slightly different.

Now try doing this reading on your own with cards that you've drawn yourself. Ask "What should this woman do about her career?" and pull three cards. Write your interpretations down in your tarot journal. It's okay if the advice you give is different than what we gave in the sample reading. Trust what the cards and your intuition are telling you, and build your own narrative from the cards you've drawn; it may well have a different ending, and that's to be expected.

Crossroads Spread

This is a six-card variation on the Past/Present/Future spread. The central card represents the matter at hand, the subject of the reading. On top of this, and rotated so that it's placed horizontally, is a card that "crosses" you, representing the challenge, obstruction, or problem being faced. Then, put a card on the left to represent the past and a card on the right to represent the future. Below the central cards, the fifth card in the spread represents the root cause of the problem, where it comes from. And finally, above the central cards, you place one last card to represent overall advice for the ideal course of action.

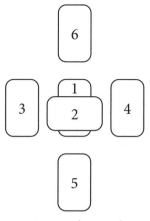

Crossroads Spread

This spread is a scaled-down version of a very famous (but somewhat difficult and unwieldy) tarot spread known as the Celtic Cross. It still provides the same basic temporal through-line as the previous spread, but it adds more information about the problem and how to solve it. The Past/Present/Future spread says, "Here's where you came from, where you are now, and where you're headed." The Crossroads spread says all of that but adds, "Here's what your problem is, where it came from, and how you should deal with it."

Decision-Making Spread

Certain kinds of questions lend themselves to specialized spreads. This is a six-card spread designed to help make a decision between two options. If there are more than two options, you can always expand this spread as necessary.

Begin by laying out three cards in a vertical line on the left-hand side of your reading space. These three cards (numbers 1, 2, and 3) represent what will happen if you choose option A. Then, lay out three more cards on the right-hand side of the reading; these three cards (numbers 4, 5, and 6) represent what will happen if you choose option B.

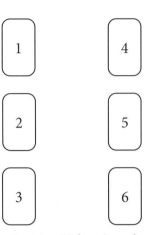

Decision-Making Spread

The three-card clusters can either be read individually (here are three separate things that will happen if you choose option A) or together (here are three features of one thing that will happen). This is largely a matter of personal preference and what feels right to you. If you opt for the former, you will interpret each card on its own according to the process we've been using so far. If you choose the latter, you'll want to look for the way the cards fit together and present a single, cohesive message. This can take time to figure out how to do, and some of the techniques we'll explore later on will make the process easier.

Heart-Shaped Relationship Spread

Some spreads rely on geometric imagery to help tell a story. This is a heart-shaped spread for questions about romantic relationships. Begin by dealing three cards in a triangle in the upper left-hand corner of the spread. These represent the first partner in the relationship: what they want, what they need, and what they offer to their partner. Then, deal three more cards in the upper right-hand corner, representing the same three things from the second partner's point of view. Finally, in the bottom center portion of your reading space, you deal three more cards in an inverted triangle. These represent the strengths of the relationship, the challenges facing the relationship, and where the relationship is going in the future.

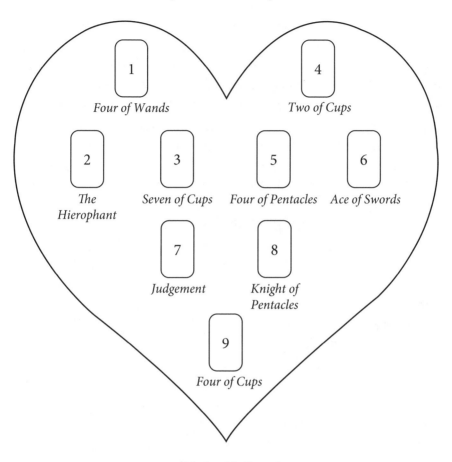

Four of Wands

Two of Cups

The
Hierophant

Seven of Cups   Four of Pentacles   Ace of Swords

Judgement

Knight of
Pentacles

Four of Cups

Relationship Spread

This reading is designed for relationships with only two partners, but it can be modified for polyamorous relationships simply by adding three more cards at the top for each additional partner. (Doing so means that the spread is no longer heart-shaped, but that's merely an aesthetic consideration.) Likewise, the spread is ideal for future-facing questions like "How will this relationship progress?" If you want to ask something slightly different, such as "What should I do to cultivate this relationship?", you might want to alter the meaning of the final card. Rather than being a forecast for the future, you could decide to have the final card represent the best course of action or advice for what you should do.

This raises an important point. *Tarot spreads can be modified to suit your needs.* The spreads included in this book and every other tarot book are working schemas to help you get the information you need out of a reading. Sometimes, the circumstances of your question are specific enough that no premade spread will exactly capture the information you want. In those cases, it's perfectly okay to adapt a spread to suit your needs. You can add cards, subtract them, or change the meaning of particular card positions in a spread. Spreads are intended to be useful and informative, so don't hesitate to adjust them as much as you have to in order to make them as informative as possible.

Designing Your Own Spread

There are far more tarot spreads than we have room to discuss in this chapter. In fact, there are entire books devoted just to tarot spreads. There's a spread for every occasion and for every possible question. However, if you're trying to perform a reading and you haven't yet found a spread you like for your question, the best thing to do is to design your own. There's no official listing of approved tarot spreads and no reason that you have to use a layout made up by someone else. Remember, a spread is just a layout of cards designed to give you more specific information about a particular question. No one knows better than you what information you need to answer your question, so no one is better qualified than you to design a spread for your reading.

When making your own spread, start by thinking about the question you're going to ask. In order for an answer to that question to be satisfactory, what information does it have to give you? What things do you have to know in order to feel like your question was fully and properly answered? Sit down and make a list of the basic points of information you need. Some of these may draw on features of other spreads, like having cards to represent the past, present, and future. Likewise, there are structural elements common to certain kinds of spreads. If you're doing a predictive reading, then you'll want to have at least one card for the future, representing the outcome of the situation. Romance and relationship readings are generally symmetrical, with the same number of cards for each partner. Decision-making readings will have at least one card per available option. And so on.

Once you have your list, take a minute to look through it and make sure it's not too bloated nor redundant. The goal here is to have *just enough* information. You don't want multiple cards that are going to tell you basically the same thing. Do some editing on your list and make sure you're happy with it. Then, figure out how you want to lay out the cards. For example, if you have some cards related to one person's thoughts and actions and some for another's, you'll probably want to group Person A's cards and Person B's cards separately. Likewise, if your spread includes a temporal progression, it's usually best to lay out those cards in order from left to right so that they're easier to follow. Find a layout that is aesthetically pleasing to you and that allows the information in your reading to flow freely. Then, the only thing left for you to do is read.

Practice Reading: A Jilted Spouse

A man comes to you for a reading because he is convinced his husband is having an affair—with the husband's boss, no less! Your querent is anguished and wants to know if there is any hope for salvaging his marriage. Design a spread that you would use with this querent. Then, shuffle your cards and perform a reading for him. Record your reading in your tarot journal.

The Non-Spread

Some tarot readers don't like to use spreads with prescribed meanings for each individual card. They find such layouts interrupt the flow of a reading and are unnecessarily constrictive. These readers prefer to pull a few cards—usually somewhere between three and six—and interpret them collectively, allowing their themes to blend together.

As an example, let's look at the three cards we drew for the Past/Present/Future spread: the Nine of Pentacles, the Four of Cups, and the Eight of Pentacles. Rather than assigning specific meanings to these cards, someone using this more freeform reading style would say that all three are aspects of the same answer to this woman's question. She asked about changing her career, and the answer to that question is a synthesis of the themes represented by these cards.

The three cards respectively represent success, stagnation, and study, so if we read them without a defined spread, then the answer to our querent's question will involve those main themes. One potential answer is that this woman would be successful if she switched careers and became a chef, but that it would be an overwhelming amount of work for her and she'd ultimately be unhappy with it. On the other end of things, we might come up with a similar answer to the one we had with the formal spread. She is unhappy despite her success, and the way forward out of that unhappiness is for her to apply herself to learning something new.

This can be confusing at first. How could the same cards mean two totally different things? If you're using this freeform reading technique rather than a spread with rigidly defined card positions, then a great deal of the interpretive process will have to rely on your intuition. Different readers might look at the same cards and get different gut-level feelings about what those cards mean. Part of reading tarot is learning to trust that your intuition is leading you in the right direction, even when there are other viable interpretations. (This is also why it's important not to kibitz on other people's readings! You might interpret things differently, but you have to trust that their intuition is guiding them correctly in their own reading.)

The choice of whether to use spreads or read more loosely is entirely a personal one. It all comes down to personal preference and the way that you feel most comfortable. Most beginners tend to like the structure and support offered by spreads, but it's worth testing yourself and trying both ways. The most important thing is that you feel you're able to get enough information out of your readings.

5
Reversed Cards

Tarot cards, as you have probably noticed by now, have pictures on them. Moreover, most of the time, those pictures are spatially oriented; there's a "right way up" and an "upside down" way for a card to be turned. Not all decks have this feature—decks with unillustrated pips usually have at least some cards in the Minor Arcana that are rotationally symmetric—but it is the norm for the vast majority of tarot decks. This introduces an interesting possibility for tarot interpretation; we can read a card differently when it appears upside down versus right side up.

This technique in tarot is referred to as reading with *reversals*; an upside-down card is said to be *reversed*. Many tarot readers choose not to read with reversals, simply turning every card upright as they draw it. Novice readers, especially, tend to balk at the idea. They already have to memorize the meanings of seventy-eight individual cards, and now they have to memorize what those cards mean when they're upside down too? To say that it's an intimidating prospect is a gross understatement. However, learning to read with reversals is much easier than it might seem at first, and it can provide a valuable level of nuance to your readings.

As with all of the techniques presented in this book, the goal of using reversals is to make your life as a reader easier, not harder. If you try them and don't like them, you are under no obligation to use them, but many readers find that they provide crucial insight into the forces at work in a reading.

Yes, But...

So how do reversals work in a reading? How are you supposed to interpret an upside-down card? To begin with, understand that *a card is the same card regardless of whether it's upright or reversed.* The key themes at play remain the same; it's simply that those themes may manifest differently in a reversed card than in an upright one. When a card appears upright in a reading, its themes manifest in full force. When it is reversed, however, those themes are somehow subverted.

I like to think of an inverted card as a message that says, "Yes, *but*..." An upright card says, "This is what's going on!" When reversed, that card is talking about the same sort of thing. It has the same subject matter, the same general content. However, it restricts that message somehow. There's something in the way, something preventing it from manifesting fully. A reversed card says, "This is more or less what's going on, *but* not quite." The central theme of the card is present, but it's stunted somehow.

Consider a card like the Ace of Pentacles. Upright, this card says that you're embarking on a new project; inverted, it says that maybe there's something new in the works, *but* it's not ready to get off the ground yet. Alternatively, you're trying to start a new project but someone else is holding it back. The central idea is still present; the card tells us that we're somewhere in the domain of newness, beginnings, investment, and so on. That's the *yes.* The *but* is that those themes are frustrated in some meaningful way: the new business idea has already been done by someone else, the investment won't profit, or the new hobby is expensive and impractical. There's a beginning at work somewhere, yes, but that's not the whole story.

A reversal can mean a variety of things, and often the other cards in a reading can help point you toward what, exactly, it signifies. For example, the reversed Ace of Pentacles combined with the Four of Pentacles might tell us that a new business is going to suffer from a lack of investors, while the reversed Ace combined with the Seven of Pentacles might mean that the business can ultimately prosper, but that prosperity is going to take a lot more work and patience than the owners had hoped for. The reversal gives you the *but* and tells you there's more information to be had, but the specifics are often left open for you to figure out—through other cards in the reading, by using your intuition, or even simply by asking your querent for more context about their situation.

A Reversed Card Is N.O.T. Itself

Here's a handy (if somewhat cheesy) mnemonic device to help with reading reversed cards. The meaning of an inverted card is N.O.T. what that card means when it's upright: Negated, Obstructed, or Tempered. Reversals in different contexts can mean any or all of these three things; figuring out which one is a matter of your personal judgment, and it's something you'll get better at with practice.

Negated

Sometimes, a reversal can signify the complete opposite of a card's ordinary meaning. If you draw a reversed card that usually represents hard work and diligence, the reversal may well mean laziness and indolence. If a card ordinarily means community and social connection, a reversal can draw out themes of isolation and loneliness. This is the truest sense in which upside-down cards are "reversals" of their upright counterparts.

Typically, this interpretation works best with cards that deal in ordinary, mundane themes rather than cards that are dramatically positive or negative. The Seven of Pentacles in reverse can easily symbolize impatience and an unwillingness to keep one's nose to the grindstone. This is because that energy is contained, somewhat, in the meaning of the upright card; patience and impatience go hand in hand. They're part of the same essence. To take our "Yes, *but …*" mentality, it makes sense to say, "Yes, we're talking about patience and hard work, *but* you're being kind of hot-headed and entitled."

A doom-and-gloom card like the Five of Pentacles in reverse, on the other hand, is unlikely to transform into a card of resplendent joy and good fortune. That's simply too far removed from the central theme of the card. It may happen occasionally, depending on the reading, but most of the time, we wouldn't say, "Yes, we're talking about hardship and suffering, *but* everything looks bright and joyful." It usually only makes sense to interpret a reversed card as negated when the negation still fits into the broader theme that the card represents.

Obstructed

Reversals can also indicate obstruction or blockage in the energy of a card—something is interfering with the card, preventing it from expressing itself the way it normally would. This could be an external circumstance, another person, or even an internal psychological condition on behalf of the person who requested the reading. A reversal can indicate that someone is of two minds about something, that they think they want what this card has to offer but that some part of them wants something different. The blockage can be out in the world or it can be from within, but something or someone is impeding this card from acting as itself.

This kind of reversal can also manifest as a temporal delay. Particularly when you draw a reversed card in the "future" or "outcome" position in a spread, it can mean that something is going to happen, but that there will be problems and delays to deal with before it does. A reversed card means blockages, difficulty, miscommunication, and frustration—but it tells us that ultimately, those things can be overcome.

Tempered

The third major way we can interpret a reversed card is that it tempers the meaning of the upright card. It's the same basic meaning, but weaker and more toned down. Where the Ten of Pentacles could represent an inheritance or an endowment, the Ten of Pentacles in reverse might represent something smaller, like a birthday present from your grandmother. Where the Nine of Pentacles is the payoff after a long period of hard work, the reversed Nine might be a minor payoff like a spa day. In this sense, reversed cards can take the same energy that we ordinarily see in a card and shrink it down to a less dramatic scale. You're still getting the same thing, but in a much smaller quantity.

This can be helpful in a reading because it shows us that not all cards are equal. If you have three cards and two of them are reversed, then the influence of the upright one is likely to be much stronger and more prodigious. The other two are still present, but they have less total effect on the outcome of the reading. Using reversals in this way allows you to see themes that are still present and relevant to the question you've asked, but that aren't the dominant forces at play.

Practice Reading: A Birthday Party

A woman comes to you for a reading about a birthday party she has been planning for her mother. She was supposed to plan the party together with her sister, but her sister makes less money than she does and was upset about the expensive venue and catering. The two of them had a falling out, and there are hurt feelings all around; your querent wants to know what she should do to fix things.

Shuffle your deck in such a way that roughly half of the cards will be reversed. (If you shuffle overhand, periodically remove a section of the deck, rotate it 180 degrees, and put it back in.) Then, do a reading for this querent, using either the Crossroads spread or a spread of your own devising. Pay particular attention to the reversed cards in the reading. How do they contribute to your understanding of what's going on? Record the reading in your tarot journal.

The Dark Side of a Card

There is another way that people sometimes choose to interpret reversals: as the dark, unpleasant, or negative aspect of a card's energy. Just about every card in the tarot deck has both positive and negative features. Some readers use reversals as a way of indicating when they should focus on the "bad" side of a card.

Personally, I don't favor this method of interpretation. I find that it skews things toward the gloomy and unpleasant. There are some cards in the deck, such as the Five of Pentacles, that already deal with suffering and misery when they're upright; choosing to interpret every reversed card as bad simply means that more than half your potential interpretations will be bleak and disheartening. Make no mistake, unpleasant themes are an inescapable part of life, and we don't want to flinch away from them in our tarot readings; sometimes we really do have to confront difficult and disheartening subjects. However, those unpleasant themes are not *all* of life, nor even most of it. We don't want to bias our readings toward sorrow and despair any more than we want to bias them toward fluff and light.

Reversals can, and sometimes do, signify the bad parts of a card, but be careful not to rely too heavily on this interpretive crutch. Remember that reversals can introduce a great deal of nuance into a reading. They often have more to say than simply, "The Star, but make it bad."

Another way to express roughly the same idea is to interpret reversed cards as imbalanced in some way. When a card is reversed, there is too much or too little of it, and that excess or lack can become a serious problem if it's left unattended. A reversal is not, in and of itself, a bad thing. However, it does need to be brought into harmony with the other cards in the reading, and if that is not done, then badness can ensue.

Identifying Blockages in a Reading

One of the most useful applications of reversals is that they allow you, as a reader, to survey the whole of a reading and identify the places where there are challenges, blockages, and obstacles to overcome. If you have a five-card spread and two of those cards are reversed (which is statistically likely), then those two cards indicate the blockages in your situation.

This is true of the cards themselves, insofar as you can say something like "The Three of Cups and the Knight of Wands appear to be problem areas," but it's also true of the spread positions that have been assigned to those cards. If you have the reversed Three of Cups in the "past" position, then even before you interpret that card, you know where there's a problem—you're clinging to something in the past. You're unable to get over something that happened in the past, and until you let go of that event, you'll be unable to move forward into the future. Then, you can look at the specifics of the Three of Cups in that position to figure out what, exactly, the nature of that past event is.

Likewise, if you have the Knight of Wands reversed in a spread position that deals with your relationship with your boss, you immediately know that's a source of trouble for you. Before you even look at the specifics of the card and identify why your relationship with your boss is a problem area, you know that it is one. You can identify the parts of a reading where there are problems, and then dive in and analyze the cards in those positions in order to understand what those problems are, where they come from, and how to fix them.

It can even be the case that someone's life is such a mess, so full of blockages and challenges and overlapping problems, that a single tarot reading won't be able to fix it. If you do a reading for someone and most—or even all—of the cards are reversed, that tells you that their life is way out of balance. They have a lot of problems with multiple different sources, and those problems need to be handled one at a time in order to be untangled effectively. A reading full of reversals is a big red warning sign: things are out of whack. Proceed with caution. (Importantly, this is only the case in a reading with several cards. If you only turn up one or two cards, it's statistically unremarkable for all of them to come up reversed.)

Used in this way, reversals can be an invaluable first-pass technique to help you identify the areas of a reading that require the most attention, the places where things are tangled up and need to be unwound. Reversed cards can show how things are out of balance, and knowing that much gives you the beginnings of a plan for how to make them right.

Practice Reading: A Struggling Student

A college student comes to you for a reading because they've been struggling to keep up with school. They're taking five classes this semester, on top of which they're working part-time at the movie theater, volunteering at a local nursing home, and participating in their school's astronomy club. They know they have too much on their plate, and their grades are suffering, but they love all of the activities they're involved in, and they don't know what they should cut.

Perform a reading for this querent, using a variation of the Decision-Making spread from chapter 4 or another spread of your choosing. Shuffle the cards in such a way that roughly half of them will be reversed. In this reading, pay particular attention to which cards are reversed and what that says about the blockages this student is experiencing in their life. Record the reading in your tarot journal.

Should You Use Reversals?

The subject of reversals is hotly debated among tarot readers. Those who like to use reversals claim that doing so allows them to see nuance and complexity in a reading, offering a wider range of potential interpretations for every card in the deck. Those who eschew reversals argue that they have that same range of potential interpretations available to them whether a card is reversed or not. Ultimately, it's a matter of what works best for you. Different readers have different styles, and the techniques that work for one person might leave another cold. That's okay.

I recommend trying reversals, at least for a little while, until you feel you've got the hang of them. Then, if you decide you don't like them, you can always drop them. However, even if you don't end up using reversals in the long run, it's good practice to learn how. Exploring the ways a card is different when reversed will help you form a deeper, more colorful understanding of that card—and that way, even if you choose to read only upright for the rest of your life, you'll have more to draw on whenever that card appears in a reading.

6
The Suit of Swords

Whereas the suit of Pentacles dealt in practical and material themes, the suit of Swords is about our minds. Cards in this suit have to do with the things we think, say, believe, doubt, and communicate to each other. The fact of the matter is that words can hurt, and our thoughts can torment us; this suit reflects those realities. The suit of Swords gets a bit of a bad rap because it contains some of the most harrowing cards in the tarot deck. However, Swords are not only negative cards; they also represent all of the positive potential that our minds can offer.

Ace of Swords

Whereas the Ace of Pentacles was the beginning of a new project, the Ace of Swords is a new idea. It is the breath of inspiration that stirs our minds and moves us to think of something new. When an inventor has been toiling in her lab for months on end trying to solve a problem and finally figures it out, the Ace of Swords is the "Eureka!" moment that accompanies her discovery. This is the moment when the clouds part and heavenly choirs start singing, where everything becomes blissfully clear and you can suddenly see the world in a totally new way.

Of course, that language sounds a bit grandiose, but we experience the Ace of Swords energy all the time. Every time we find a more efficient way to load the dishwasher or a different route to work, every time we find a solution to a problem and our eyes light up, and every time we have a new idea, big or small, we are experiencing the energy of the Ace of Swords. This card is the essence of *having an idea*. It is pure reason, the function of our minds applied to the understanding of the world around us. The Ace of Swords represents clarity, insight, inspiration, and truth.

Not all ideas are good, and sometimes we have a flash of inspiration that proves to be misguided; our novel dishwasher-loading technique results in half a dozen chipped plates, our new route to work gets us stuck in traffic, or our magic-bullet solution solves one problem but creates another. This sort of thing happens all the time. The Ace of Swords is the process of thinking and innovating, and unfortunately, innovation requires sifting through a lot of lousy ideas in order to find one good one. The Ace is just the starting point, the initial idea that gets us going; where that idea takes us is an open question. Sometimes it'll be a road to success, and other times we'll find ourselves back at our starting point, doing everything over again.

Nevertheless, the Ace of Swords at its best represents the sheer wonder and power of the human mind: everything we're capable of accomplishing just through thinking. It is the cold beauty of mathematics and logic, the knockdown persuasion of a well-crafted argument, and the feeling of delight we get when we've finally cracked a tough puzzle. This is the card that brings everything together and makes us say, "Oh, *now* I see. It all makes sense." When the Ace of Swords turns up in a reading, we get a glimpse into the machinery of the universe, a prized moment of clear understanding that helps us orient ourselves. The Ace of Swords gives us an idea of what it's all really about, and with that idea, we can then move forward and act based on the insight we've gained.

Two of Swords

The Twos in tarot are all about duality and reciprocity. In the intellectual suit of Swords, we find the duality of choice. This card presents us with a decision—and decision's twin, indecision. This is the card of being "of two minds" about something. It's about having two paths in front of us and being forced to choose between them, even when we're unsure of ourselves. Choices can be overwhelming—agonizing even. What if we choose wrong? How are we supposed to know which option is best? Are we really qualified to make the big decisions that are laid before us? Do we have enough information? Despite all of these questions, the Two of Swords sits us down at the table and commands us to *choose*. A decision has to be made, and we have to be the ones to make it, even if that decision is imperfect. We cannot allow ourselves to be paralyzed by indecisiveness.

The image in this card is a blindfolded woman holding two swords across her chest. The swords are her two options, representing the decision she must make. The blindfold, however, restricts her knowledge. She cannot know for sure how each choice will pan out or what the exact consequences of her decision will be. She can make an educated guess, sure, but ultimately she doesn't know. She has to make a choice between the two swords—two options that feel roughly the same in her hands—and, to a certain extent, she has to make that choice blind.

The Two of Swords often appears in situations where what we most want to do is to suspend judgment. When we're making a high-stakes decision and we're terrified of getting it wrong, we want to postpone the part where we actually choose. We don't want to put our money on the line. Instead, we perpetually search for more information, for better forecasts, and for certainty about what the right choice really is. The Two of Swords tells us that we can postpone judgment no longer. We have all the information that is going to be available to us, and our decision isn't going to get any easier or any clearer than it already is. Now is the time to choose. Whatever the consequences of our choice may be, we can—and must—live with them, but not deciding is not an option.

That's not to say we should rush to judgment. The Two of Swords is still a rational, airy card. It's still rooted in careful thought and consideration. We should evaluate our options, analyze all the information available to us, and make a choice after honest and fair deliberation. However, it is also our duty to remember that deliberation is only a part of the process. At the end of the road, after all the deliberating and weighing of our options, there is still a judgment to be made. We should be balanced and consider all perspectives, but having considered them, we must then pick our path forward and follow it.

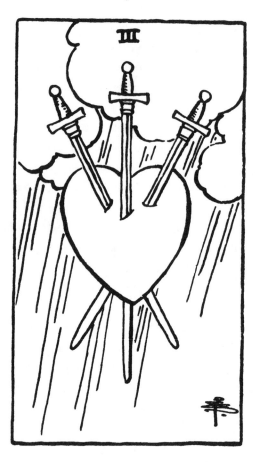

Three of Swords

The Three of Swords is the single most visually evocative card in the Minor Arcana. A bloody heart is pierced through by three blades, set against a dismal background of clouds and rain. This is a card of sorrow and loss. It's the feeling you get when someone breaks your heart and you feel like you've been stabbed in the chest. The Three of Swords is a card of wounds—not old wounds that have healed with time, mind you, but wounds that are still fresh, raw, and bleeding. This is the card that makes us hurt.

I warned at the beginning of this chapter that the suit of Swords has a bad reputation amongst tarot readers, and the Three is one of the chief reasons why. Tarot encompasses the whole range of human experience, from the good to the bad, and in the Three of Swords, we get an unflinching acknowledgment of the bad. This is a card of *pain*. There's no two ways about it; sometimes we hurt. Our wounds may come from others, either intentionally or unintentionally. The Three of Swords can be the pain that comes from a bad breakup, from having someone lash out and say mean things to you, or from the death of a loved one. It can be the result of malice, or it can just be a bad situation where somebody gets wounded despite everyone trying their best. On the other hand, the pain of the Three of Swords can be more internal, reflecting physical or psychological self-harm.

Importantly, this kind of pain doesn't last forever. It can't; humans are built to adapt. As intense and raw as our wounds feel when they're first inflicted, over time we learn how to live with them. Some of them may heal over so well that we forget the pain altogether. Others stay with us for our whole lives, leaving scars that sometimes reopen and hit us with a fresh wave of grief. Even the deepest and most lasting wounds will heal in some capacity, though. When we're confronted with the immediacy and intensity of our pain, it can sometimes feel impossible to go on living our lives, but over time, that pain will fade, and we will find some way to return to life. Our hearts always have the capacity to heal, even when it doesn't feel that way.

This doesn't negate the reality or depth of the pain we may feel. It is simply a promise that pain is not the end. When someone or something breaks our hearts, it is important to acknowledge that heartbreak and honor it by allowing ourselves to feel it fully. However, it's just as important to honor ourselves by understanding that we can and will heal, given time. It's okay to cry and scream and fall to pieces. That's what you *should* do. Process your pain honestly, however long it takes to work through. Don't let anyone make you feel like you're taking too long or like your pain is undeserved. But when the time comes, allow yourself to live again. It's okay to heal, just as it's okay to be in pain.

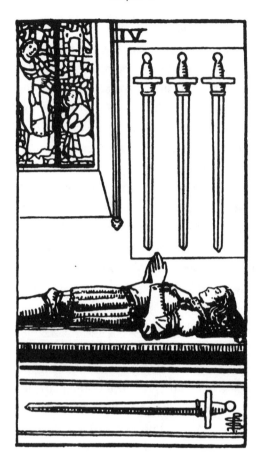

Four of Swords

After the harrowing experience of the Three of Swords, we need a respite, and we find it in the Four. This card depicts a tomb with a sarcophagus carved with the effigy of a figure folding their hands in prayer. It is a card of stillness, quiet, and much-needed rest. The Four of Swords is not a spa treatment; it doesn't pamper us or surround us with luxury. Rather, it gives us shelter from the onslaughts of the world. It is a brief moment to recuperate from the hardships of day-to-day life. It's a chance to catch our breath, orient ourselves, and recover before we dive back in to the fray.

We all need to rest sometimes. If we don't make space for ourselves to rest, that space will impose itself upon us; we fall asleep at the wheel, our eyes glaze over at work and we can't focus on what we're doing, or we catch a cold and find ourselves stuck in bed despite our protestations. The Four of Swords is the card that forces us to acknowledge our need for rest. It grabs us by the shoulders and screams, "Take a break before you work yourself to death!"

Life on either side of the Four of Swords—both before and after—is a whirlwind. We have problems to solve, we get in arguments, and we hurt people and they hurt us. We have to deal with living in a world that is often unfair and unkind to us. The Four of Swords is the brief moment of serenity, the opportunity to walk away from all the things that harangue us, just for a little while. It doesn't solve our problems for us; they're still waiting when we go back to normal life. However, the Four of Swords gives us a little bit of breathing room. It gives us just enough space to calm down, feel safe, and screw our heads on right. That way, when we do return to our problems, we can see them a bit more clearly and handle them more effectively.

The Four of Swords demands rest, but it is not license to walk away from our problems permanently. The challenges facing us in life do still need to be confronted. Our purpose in taking a break should not be to escape our life altogether. The goal here is a tactical withdrawal, not a retreat. We want to escape ordinary life for just a little while so that we can destress and recuperate, then return refreshed and renewed. We take some time off from our responsibilities so that we can handle them better when we return, but the return is a crucial part of that process. The Four of Swords tells you to seek out a moment of stillness, not to live your life on a perpetual vacation.

Five of Swords

The Five of Swords is a card of being slighted, cheated, and cut down. Here we see a figure fighting against four others who are teaming up to defeat him. This card—another unpleasant one from the suit of Swords—is all about those times when you feel you just can't win. No matter what you do and no matter how hard you try, you can't catch a break. The rules of the game are unfair and the deck is stacked against you. You could do everything perfectly and still end up failing, through no fault of your own.

The lesson of the Five of Swords is a hard one, but it's one we've all learned at some point in our lives: life isn't fair. Sometimes people undermine us and take advantage of us. Sometimes we find ourselves victims of other people's dishonesty and malice, and there's nothing we can do to stop it. The Swords in tarot often deal with themes of thought and communication, so the Five of Swords in a reading may represent gossip or an unearned bad reputation. It can be much broader than that, though, and can represent any unfair situation, whether that unfairness is deliberately constructed by someone else or just an unhappy accident of the universe.

Moreover, sometimes the Five of Swords can be a gentle warning about our own behavior, an indication that we are being unfair to someone else. We're all capable of acting poorly. We all occasionally say or do hurtful things, talk about people behind their backs, or shortchange someone and then try to justify it to ourselves. Sometimes, the Five of Swords can appear not as an indication that others are being unfair to you, but that you are being unfair to them. It can hold up a mirror to your own behavior and show you when you are being nasty and mean-hearted, even if you think your actions are justified.

How, then, do we deal with the Five of Swords? How do we handle conflict in situations where there's no winning outcome for us? One important lesson from this card is that sometimes the best thing to do is accept our unfair circumstances, let them go, and move on to the next thing. Take the loss, lick your wounds, and focus your energy elsewhere, reorienting yourself toward something you *can* win.

If the Five of Swords is a social situation, accept that there are some people who will never be on your side no matter how hard you try to prove yourself to them; there are other people who are more worth your time and energy. If it's a project or investment, cut your losses and move on to something more fruitful. There's no point in digging in your heels to fight a losing battle. The Five of Swords is a difficult card, and no one hopes to see it in a reading, but it can give us valuable information. If we're stuck to something that can't succeed, it's important to know; with that knowledge, we can then take action and set ourselves up for success elsewhere.

Six of Swords

The Sixes in tarot are cards of redistribution, equilibrium, and reevaluation. After the hard lessons of the first half of the suit (and with even harder lessons yet to come), the Six of Swords is a moment of balance where we take inventory of our lives and shift our perspectives. This is a card of learning, growth, and reflection. In the card image, we see two figures in a boat being ferried across a river to the far shore. They are quite literally moving on, and when they look back at where they were before, they will have a new point of view. The Six of Swords invites us to change our perspective, to think about our lives from a new vantage point and consider things we might not have seen previously.

This card is all about intellectual growth and change. Our ideas shift as we learn new things. We assess what we thought we knew, and we change our beliefs in light of new evidence. Information moves us forward, makes us better, and helps us mature intellectually—so much so that we often cringe when looking back at the things we used to believe and the people we used to be, asking ourselves, *Did I really think that way?*

The Six of Swords invites us to reflect, reconsider, and reevaluate our worldview. This can be intellectual and scholastic, but it can also be more personal: a reassessment of our values, prejudices, or choices. With the Six of Swords, we have an opportunity to think critically about ourselves and the place we inhabit in the world—and then to initiate change. We take inventory of who we are and of what our lives are like, and if we don't like what we see, we have the opportunity to make changes in order to grow in a new direction. The ferry is waiting for us, with a ferryman ready to take us to the other side of the river; it is up to us to decide that we want to move forward.

Change can be scary, and often we're reluctant to let go of the attitudes and ideas that are comfortable to us. The process of introspection, of critically engaging with ourselves and trying to change our old habits and beliefs, requires an extraordinary measure of courage and self-honesty, and not everyone wants to make the commitment required by that process. But the Six of Swords tells us not to cling to that which no longer serves us. If we can muster up the courage to change, we'll be better off in the long run. If we can manage to get on that ferry and cross over to the other side of the river, we'll be grateful for the perspective we gain when we arrive at the shore.

Seven of Swords

In the Seven of Swords, we encounter themes of trickery, dishonesty, and dissembling. Here we see a thief stealing a bundle of swords, looking over his shoulder to make sure no one is following him. This is, fundamentally, a dishonest and evasive card, one that avoids direct confrontation and instead prefers to sneak away in the middle of the night. In the most literal sense, this card can represent lying, cheating, and stealing. More broadly, it points to things that are left unsaid, things that we keep hidden because we're afraid of the consequences of voicing them. The Seven of Swords sneaks and dissembles rather than confronting its problems directly.

The Seven of Swords can also indicate that you are being dishonest with yourself. We all remember our own private version of events, and we put a bit of a subconscious spin on them; that's just part of being human. Your side of a story will never be exactly the same as someone else's, and that's okay. It's normal and excusable. However, it's still important to confront our subconscious biases and to try to be as honest as possible with ourselves. When our private narrative diverges too far from reality, we need to take a long look in the mirror and reassess. The Seven of Swords can appear as a warning to that effect.

Note that this card isn't always malicious, nor even a bad thing. It's often the case that the evasive, dissembling tactics of the Seven of Swords are a defense mechanism; when someone feels unsafe or insecure, they are more likely to lie and conceal things in an attempt to protect themselves—consciously or unconsciously. The Seven of Swords helps us identify that insecurity so that we can work through it and express ourselves in a more honest, sincere, and trusting way. If the evasiveness represented by this card is a response to an unhealthy or unsafe environment, that's a sign that you need to change your environment or leave it so that you can be healthy and safe.

Sometimes a head-on approach is not a recipe for success; there are plenty of problems in life that can't be solved directly, no matter how much we might wish otherwise. In those cases, the Seven of Swords is a means to an end, a mask you wear while you're playing the role you need to play. In this light, the Seven of Swords can be a card of tact and diplomacy, where you avoid saying the thing you really mean in order to arrive at a positive outcome. Never forget, though, that the goal is ultimately to be able to remove that mask. Wearing it in the short term is sometimes necessary, but wearing it in the long term is untenable. Sometimes tact is required, but don't let it overstep itself and become outright lying and deceit.

Eight of Swords

The cards in the suit of Swords all deal, in one way or another, with our thoughts and perceptions. In the Eight of Swords, we see the way that those thoughts can limit and confine us. A blindfolded figure stands on the beach, encaged on all sides by swords stuck into the sand. If we take these swords to be representative of her thoughts, then the meaning of this card leaps out at us. The Eight of Swords is about being a prisoner to your own thoughts. This card shows up when we feel trapped and helpless, caught in a situation that we can't get out of. It's a card of confinement, whether that confinement is a literal, physical prison or a more abstract intellectual or emotional one.

Importantly with this card, we are often not nearly as trapped as we feel like we are. The figure on the Eight of Swords actually has plenty of room around her; she just can't escape her cage because of her blindfold. There *is* a way out, but the woman in the card simply hasn't found it yet. Moreover, once she does find her way free, she can wield the very swords that had kept her trapped and use them to her own ends. What confines her can be made into a weapon that helps free her.

The counterpart to imprisonment is liberation, and in the Eight of Swords we see that those two things are much more similar than we thought. The things that bind and oppress us, the things that make us feel caught and help-less, can be the very tools of our liberation. If we can learn how to use them, they can set us free. No matter how helpless we feel in the face of the things that oppress and confine us, there is hope for liberation, and the source of that hope is often where we least expect it: in the nature of our oppression and confinement. If we can truly understand what's limiting us, then we can learn how to use it to our advantage—to pick up the swords that surround us and brandish them ourselves.

The Eight of Swords is simultaneously a card of helplessness and of power, of impotence and of action. It appears in a reading when we feel stuck and don't believe that there is anything we can do to escape our situation or make it better. Nonetheless, it promises, there is a path open to us—we just have to find it. Often, the best way to find it is by examining the circumstances that constrain us in depth. No cage is perfectly built, and if we fully understand our prisons (literal or metaphorical), then we can see the weaknesses in them that will allow us to break free. Understanding, insight, and analysis are the keys to reclaiming autonomy and agency.

Nine of Swords

As we draw near the end of the suit of Swords, all of the anxieties and unquiet thoughts we've found throughout the suit begin to come to a head. In the Nine of Swords, we see an anguished figure sitting up in bed in the middle of the night with swords hanging ominously over them. This card represents anxiety, self-doubt, fear, insecurity, and the sleepless nights that come with all of the above. In the Nine of Swords, our thoughts get the better of us, and we fall into despair.

Although our fears take over in this card, we would do well to remember that fears are not reality. The Nine of Swords is a card of anxiety, of the countless "What if?" scenarios that play out in our heads when we're left alone with our thoughts, but anxiety does not tell us the way things really are. Rather, it tells us the worst-case scenario, the way we fear that things might be. It lies to us and makes everything seem worse than it actually is. The Nine of Swords is the card that, in childhood, makes the shadows in your bedroom seem bigger and gives you the feeling of cold dread in your stomach as you wonder if maybe there's a monster under your bed after all. In adulthood, our anxieties are more mundane, but they're just as insubstantial. They're the monsters that we imagine under the bed; when we turn on the light and look for them, they melt away, and we see that they were never there to begin with.

That said, simply telling yourself *It's all in my head* doesn't make your fears or doubts go away. If it did, none of us would ever struggle with anxiety in the first place. Fear is not reality, but it can feel real, and it can take a very real toll on our quality of life. The point of the Nine of Swords, then, is not to dismiss our anxieties out of hand or to tell us that we shouldn't be anxious over things we're just imagining, because we often don't have a choice in the matter. Rather, the Nine of Swords tells us to acknowledge and process the complex knot of fear, doubt, panic, and worry that we experience.

We cannot magically make our troubled thoughts go away, but we can accept that we have them and that they affect our lives. Then, having acknowledged them, we can begin the process of working through them, untangling anxiety from reality and putting those thoughts to rest one by one. This is a difficult process, and it requires a great deal of self-honesty, reflection, and compassion for yourself, as well as support from others. The goal is not to rid yourself of fear entirely, but to work through your fears so that they don't overwhelm you or keep you from living your life.

Ten of Swords

In every suit of the Minor Arcana, the Ten is the card of culmination and completion where we finally see all the disparate forces of the suit brought together. In the suit of Swords, which is so full of anguish and sorrow, the Ten proves to be a card of disaster and ruin. All the fears, all the pain, and all the unfairness and injustice we've confronted throughout the suit of Swords are brought together and made manifest in the Ten of Swords. This is the card where everything goes wrong.

The Ten of Swords depicts a figure lying facedown, stabbed in the back and bleeding to death. It's a card of betrayal, loss, and ruin. The sky in the background is heavy and dark. Looking at this card, we see a desolate scene with no saving grace and no hope. The Ten of Swords is, without a doubt, one of the most devastating cards in the deck, if not *the* most. With most cards in tarot (even the painful ones), there is a lesson to be learned, a plan of action, and a way to cope. This card, however, offers none of that. In the Ten of Swords, everything we've been working for comes to ruin, everything we've been fearing comes to reality, and there is nothing we can do about it. This is the card where all we can do is give up hope.

Understandably, nobody likes this card. No one wants to be told they're going to fail, or that they'll get stabbed in the back. No one wants to be presented with a bleak vision of the future where there's nothing they can do to make it better. Nonetheless, the Ten of Swords is an important card to have in the deck. Just as there are cards of unmitigated success and joy, there must also be cards of loss and despair. Tarot encompasses the entirety of human experience. Whether we're using tarot to look toward the future or at ourselves, we have to be prepared for the possibility that we might not like what we see. The future may well hold suffering and despair, and if it does, the Ten of Swords exists to give us warning.

The real test, then, is what we do afterward. If you know you're going to fail—and fail spectacularly and painfully—do you still have the strength to pick yourself up afterward and start over? In the Ten of Swords, everything goes to pieces, but what matters most is what you choose to do next. Despite the best-laid plans of mice and men, we can still find our lives in shambles. But once it's all over, we have the choice to sift through the rubble, to try to find anything we can salvage, and then to begin anew. Tarot moves cyclically, and every ending is followed by a beginning; even after the disastrous Ten of Swords, we have the opportunity to pursue a fresh start. With this card, we lose everything, but having lost it all, we can still start over from scratch—if we can find the strength to do so.

PART III

EMOTIONAL

7

Intuition and Imagery

Up to this point, we've touched on the idea that tarot reading relies on your intuition, but we haven't gone in depth about what *intuition* means or how you're supposed to use it. Intuition is a tricky thing to define. More than anything, it's an ineffable feeling of rightness, of knowing in your gut what a card means. It's the feeling you get when you look at a card and, without being able to explain why, you have a feeling about how you should interpret it—an instinct sitting at the edge of your consciousness that edges away if you try to examine it too closely. Intuition is the prickly feeling on the back of your neck that tells you you're in danger when you walk past a dark alleyway or that urge to make a lucky bet when you're normally not a gambler. It's a driving force of human action that can never explain itself; when intuition guides us, we simply *know*, without reasoning or justification.

In tarot reading, we harness intuition to help guide us in our interpretation of the cards. As you're beginning to discover by now, each card has a range of potential interpretations associated with it, some of which are blatantly contradictory. The Five of Swords can mean that you're being cheated or that you're cheating someone else; the Six of Pentacles can incline you to give to others or to accept charity that's offered to you. How are you supposed to know which way to interpret a card, especially across readings for different people who have their own unique circumstances?

The answer is intuition. Some readers are highly intuitive and choose never to memorize the "official" meanings of the cards, instead using the tarot simply as a gateway to unlock intuitive answers to any querent's question. Other readers, including myself, prefer a more structured approach, applying their intuition in the context of formal study. Regardless of which kind of reader you are, *all* tarot readers rely on intuition to some extent.

Intuition is the key that unlocks a tarot reading. It's the reason tarot is an art and not a science. A tarot reading is not static and computational. Rather, it is dynamic and interactive. It is a story that is told organically by the cards, the querent, and the reader, all working together. The process of interpreting a tarot spread has a component that is human and subjective; there is no universal formula that you can plug into a tarot reading, such that the Three of Swords in reverse plus the Chariot and the Knight of Pentacles always means XYZ or ABC.

Your intuition is that human component, the thing that makes a reading quintessentially *yours*—so that when you give a reading about a particular question to a particular person, no one else could have given that same reading, even if they had turned up the exact same cards. Your intuition is a personal guide, something that you and only you have privileged access to. Learning to trust it will help you tell better, more accurate, more meaningful stories through the tarot.

Practice Reading: Developing Intuition

Because intuition is, by nature, nonrational and nonconscious, it's not something you can really be taught. We all naturally have intuitive faculties; learning how to use them is largely a matter of getting out of your own way. The conscious part of your mind will downplay intuition. It will tell you that it's irrational, that you're just making lucky guesses, predicting based on probabilities, making up wild stories, or cold-reading other people's body language. To learn how to use intuition in a tarot reading, you need to temporarily shut off your conscious mind and trust the inner voice, the part of you that says, *This is the truth, but I don't know why.*

Shuffle your cards and ask a question. Set a timer for fifteen seconds (no more), then pull three cards without using a spread. For the purposes of this exercise, you are *not* allowed to look up the meanings of the cards you draw, in this or any other book. Instead, you have until your timer runs out to look at the cards and form your impression of them. Then, when your time is up, you have to give the answer to your question based on your intuitive response to the cards you drew. Say your answer aloud or write it down; this will force you to articulate it, even if you're unsure of yourself. When you're done, record your reading in your tarot journal.

The first time you try this exercise, you will likely feel far out of your comfort zone. You're a novice tarot reader—how can you possibly interpret a reading in only fifteen seconds, especially with cards you're not allowed to look up? The point is for you to *stop thinking*. Trust your gut. What's your first impression of these cards and what they're trying to tell you? Learning to identify and trust that feeling is the key to developing and applying your intuition as a tarot reader. Keywords and pre-written interpretations of the cards, spreads, elemental correspondences of the suits, and all other intellectual techniques can add depth and nuance to your tarot reading, but the core of the answer will always be in that first, reflexive reaction you have upon seeing the cards. Trust that, and you won't go astray.

Reading through Imagery

Intuitive reading is all about establishing a personal relationship with the cards, independent of what anyone else has to say. When you pull a card, what does it mean *to you*? You'll likely see things in it that no one else does, and those things are key to offering your own unique take on any tarot reading you give. One of the most personal ways to connect with your deck is to do a deep dive into the symbolism and imagery of the cards you draw. Remember, the images depicted on the cards are supposed to depict scenes that connect with the card meanings in order to make it easier for you to tell your story. By connecting with the card imagery, you can identify the major motifs of your story without ever looking at a book.

Pull a card at random from your deck. Spend a few minutes looking at it, scrutinizing every detail. Are there human figures in the card? What are they doing? Do they look happy? Upset? Weary? Confused? If there are multiple people, how are they interacting with each other? Does their relationship look loving and harmonious, or is there conflict? What does their body language tell you?

Now look at the other images in the card. What kind of a landscape is in the background? Is it lush and fertile, or barren and desolate? Are there houses and buildings, or is the scenery more natural? Take particular note of any prominent objects or animals in the scene. What do these images symbolize to you? For example, a fox might suggest cleverness (someone sneaky is "sly as a fox"), while a lion symbolizes courage. A butterfly emerging from its chrysalis could signify transformation; a cluster of eggs in a nest could signify the promise of birth and new beginnings.

In short, you're looking for the images themselves to tell you what the card means. Assume that every detail of a card's imagery was put there deliberately by the artist in order to help you understand the symbolic meaning of the card. Look at each part of the scene depicted in this card and ask yourself, *What does this mean in a deeper sense?* Nothing in tarot is ever one-dimensional. Everything has multiple layers of potential meaning to it, and your role as a reader is to uncover those layers.

Six of Cups

Take the card above, for example. We haven't yet talked about how to interpret this card, but just by looking at the image, you can get a sense of the major themes. In this card, we see children at play. The choice of children, rather than adults, tells us right away that the card connects somehow to youth, childhood, and innocence. These children are exuberant and joyful, playing with each other. They are enclosed in a garden, safe from the harms of the outside world. This is, therefore, not a card of conflict and strife; rather, it has a sense of playfulness, connection, and contentment. The children may well be siblings, so this card potentially signifies a familial connection of some kind as well—an idea that is reinforced by the glimpse of their home in the background. The cups in this card are full of blooming flowers, reminiscent of springtime; again, this symbolism shows us youth and joy.

All of these images together tell us what the card means before we even think to look up its interpretation. The imagery of the card gives us a feeling, a deep sense of what the card means, that takes precedence over any formal process of interpretation. Imagery varies across different decks, which means that the same card might require slightly different interpretations from one deck to another. That's okay! What matters is that you're finding connection and meaning in your cards. We said in chapter 1 that the most important part of picking a tarot deck is finding one with imagery that speaks to you; as a reader, all you have to do is listen.

It's also crucial to note that two people might look at the same card and find radically different meanings. A card that looks peaceful to you might seem stifling to someone else; a card that you find competitive and full of strife might strike someone else as an expression of vitality and passion. Different readers can see the same spread and derive radically different messages from it. That does not undermine their respective skills as readers. Rather, it means that their intuitive responses to the cards lead them in different directions. The message that you need to get out of a reading (or, if you're reading for someone else, the message your querent needs to get) is not the same as the message someone else needs to get. Trust that your intuition is leading you in the right direction for *your* reading, just as another reader's intuition will lead them in the right direction for theirs.

Whatever cards turn up in your reading, they're the right ones for that question at that time. Likewise, the way that your intuition guides you to interpret them is the right interpretation for those cards at that time. Remember, reading intuitively is mostly a matter of getting out of your own way. Trust yourself, and trust your response to the cards. Other people may have different responses, but when you're in the thick of a reading, what matters is *your* intuitive response—not anyone else's.

Practice Reading: Will She Call?

You meet a woman named Shawna who wants a reading about her love life. A coworker recently set Shawna up on a blind date with a woman named Carmen. They had a lovely dinner, Shawna gave Carmen her phone number, and Carmen promised to call—but a week later, Shawna still hasn't heard from Carmen. Shawna wants to know if Carmen is actually going to call her, or if she should move on and forget about this date. If Carmen is not going to call, Shawna wants to know why. Did she do something wrong? She thought the date went well, and not hearing from Carmen has left her feeling hurt and confused.

Do a reading for Shawna using any spread of your choosing. For this reading, *do not* look up the interpretations of any of the cards. Try to rely only on the imagery and symbolism of the cards you draw in conjunction with your intuition. When you are done, record your reading in your tarot journal.

Getting Specific

One of the great advantages of intuitive reading is that it allows you to make hyper-specific interpretations that aren't necessarily offered in tarot books. Sometimes when you're reading, you'll get a flash of insight based on an image or a gut feeling about one of the cards. It might be a specific detail of a situation ("Your business partner is lying to you"), the identity of a person ("The Queen of Wands here represents your mother"), or a definitive yes-or-no answer to your querent's question ("You're not going to get this job"). Often, these specificities feel like they come out of nowhere. You'll get an idea pressing at the back of your head, something that you can't shake, telling you that the cards mean *this particular thing*.

These intuitive flashes might be a matter of imagery that strikes you in a particular way; for example, maybe you draw the Seven of Swords and the central figure looks just like your querent's business partner, or you draw the Queen of Wands and she looks like your querent's mother. Alternatively, your intuition may simply be a matter of honing in on one specific interpretation out of an array of many possibilities; you know from this book that the Seven of Swords represents prevarication, and then your intuition tells you *who*, specifically, is doing the prevaricating.

However, intuition can just as easily be totally inexplicable. Your gut might guide you to an interpretation that's completely beyond the scope of the "normal" themes associated with a card. When that happens, trust yourself. When your instincts lead you to offer a specific prediction or interpretation in a tarot reading, you should go with what feels right, even if you can't find a rational explanation for why that interpretation makes sense to you.

It's perfectly understandable to be hesitant about offering such detailed readings. It's a lot scarier to say "Your business partner is lying to you" than "There's a general theme of dishonesty and miscommunication at work here." The more detailed you get in your readings, the easier it is to confirm whether you were right or wrong after the fact—and nobody likes facing the possibility that they could be wrong. All tarot readers face the temptation to retreat into platitudes and the general statements that will almost always prove true regardless of a querent's particular circumstances, things like "You need to work on yourself right now" or "Not everyone is communicating openly." Retreating into vague interpretations can feel safer, but the more specific you make your readings, the more useful they'll actually be.

As a tarot reader, you want to provide fresh insight; you want to tell your querent something they didn't already know. Detail and specificity make a tarot reading shine. It takes time to learn how to identify the gut feeling that allows you to give concrete details in a tarot reading, and you're sure to make your fair share of mistakes, particularly as a novice reader who is still learning how to distinguish genuine intuition from mere expectations or wishful thinking. That's okay. Making mistakes is part of the learning process, as with any other skill.

To hone your intuition, I'd encourage you to try to identify at least one specific detail in every reading you perform. If you do predictive readings, try to make your readings concrete and verifiable; if you avoid predicting the future, you can still give details about someone's current situation, the options available to them, or the people they're interacting with. Record all of these details in your tarot journal, and return to your recorded readings after the fact to take note of where your interpretations were accurate and where you missed the mark.

Over time, you'll learn to identify the feeling that comes with the accurate readings—that's the feeling of your intuition. By forcing yourself into specificity and keeping track of your successes and failures, you can find the common thread that ties your accurate predictions together. Intuition is difficult to explain and nigh impossible to learn just by reading about it in a book; the best way to acquire a sense of it is to perform as many readings as possible, make predictions, and gain your own experiential sense of what a successful prediction feels like. Eventually, you'll reach a point with your intuition where you know it when you feel it.

Tarot as Storytelling

This is the single most important lesson of this entire book: *reading tarot is telling a story.* You are reading for yourself or for a querent, the protagonist of the story. That protagonist is set in a particular environment and is faced with a central conflict—the subject of the reading. They have strengths, allies, and tools available to help them deal with that conflict, but at the same time, there are also weaknesses, enemies, and obstacles. As a tarot reader, you're bringing all of these things together to tell one coherent narrative. Depending on what your querent wants to know, you might focus on some parts of it—for example, *How does the story end?* or *What is the source of the conflict?*—but the whole story is still present in the background.

The most important thing you do as a reader, then, is figure out what story you're telling. Each card you draw gives you one piece of information, a snapshot of one part of the story. Your job is to bring all those snapshots together, put them in the right order, and fill in the blanks between them in order to produce a single coherent narrative. When you look at a reading, you want to identify:

- The source of conflict. What is the central problem? Where are the challenges or tensions in the cards you've drawn?
- How that conflict will be resolved. What resources are available to solve the problems the reading presents? Which cards can offer solutions?

- The main people involved. Who are the actors affecting the situation? How do their motivations or actions interact with each other—either promoting or obstructing each other's goals?
- The temporal sequence of events. What happened in the past? What's going to happen in the future?
- The causal relations between events. The future does not exist in isolation; it flows forth from the past in a complicated sequence of cause and effect. How do the events in your reading affect and depend on each other? How is card X a result of card Y?

This sounds like a lot, and it can be intimidating, but it's really much more straightforward than it might seem. Simply put, our goal is to read the cards *together*, to take the reading as a whole rather than just interpreting each card individually. We want to learn how to look simultaneously at the details and the big picture so that we don't miss the forest for the trees.

Spatial Relations

You can learn a great deal about the thematic relationships between the cards just by looking at their spatial relations. Where a card lies in your reading can tell you something about the role it plays in the overall story—how its individual theme weaves into the larger narrative you are trying to make.

In much of the English-speaking world, we think about time in spatial terms. Time flows along a horizontal axis, so if we're telling a story through pictures, we start out on the left and progress through time as we move to the right. This is a cultural convention that comes from the way English is written and read; we are accustomed to following stories from left to right, and we've come to associate that directional axis with the arrow of time. Native speakers of languages with different writing conventions may conceptualize time as flowing from right to left instead.

In a tarot reading, you can leverage this cultural association. As a rule of thumb, the cards you draw can be ordered in time depending on where they sit horizontally in your reading. The more to the left a card is, the farther it is in the past; the more to the right, the farther in the future. Just looking at the distribution of cards along the horizontal axis can give you a sense of the progression of events in your reading. This helps you identify which events come first and which follow after.

Likewise, cards that are spatially located in the center of a reading are often going to be thematically central as well. The closer to the center a card is, the more important it is. Central cards are crucial to our understanding of what's going on in a reading; often, the cards at the center represent the heart of the matter, and cards on the periphery serve as an aid in their interpretation. When you're feeling overwhelmed by the amount of information you have in a reading and you don't know where to begin, start at the center and work your way out. The central cards in your reading are in the spotlight. They're the stars of the show, and every other card is playing off them. If you get to an outer card and struggle to understand its significance, you can always gain insight by thinking about how it relates to the themes on display in the center.

Finally, you can look at the vertical axis of your reading, as well. Things at the bottom of a reading tend to be hidden, obscure, and unconscious. They represent the things you don't know: subconscious motivations, the root causes of a problem, secrets being kept, backroom dealings, or anything that is private (either in your own life or someone else's). The farther up we move along the vertical axis, the more out in the open a card is. Cards at the very top of your reading space represent things that are obvious, public, and well-known: the conscious mind, analysis about a situation, current events, the political climate, direct communication with other people, and anything having to do with public life. Looking at the vertical dimension of a spread can help you identify what's being kept hidden and how that affects the circumstances of your reading.

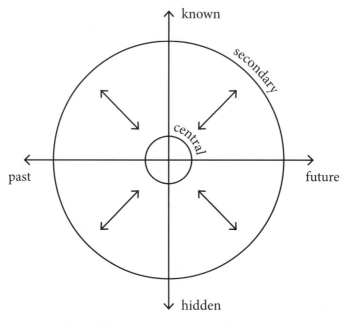

Vertical, horizontal, center-periphery axes

These principles can be used in any reading to identify how the themes of the individual cards fit together to form a larger whole; indeed, many tarot spreads (such as the Crossroads spread from chapter 4) are designed to incorporate these principles. A card on its own tells you that a particular theme is at play, but when you consider where that card lies relative to the rest of the reading, you can begin to understand the specifics of how its themes manifest. The Six of Swords in the bottom right-hand corner of a reading will have a different impact than the Six of Swords sitting dead center. Every card in your reading is a part of a larger whole, and your job as a tarot reader is to fit those parts together in the right way so that you can see what the whole is supposed to look like. Examining the spatial relations between the cards is a helpful way to begin to see the work that each card is contributing toward the meaning of the overall spread.

Practice Reading: Using Card Placement

Ask a question of your choosing, then draw nine cards. Lay these cards out in a three-by-three grid. Using the spatial principles you've just learned, how do you interpret this reading? What is the central issue at stake? What's the progression of events from past to future? What information is out in the open, and what's kept hidden?

Now, setting aside the rest of the deck, take those nine cards and reshuffle them. Deal them out again in a three-by-three grid, in a new and random order. You now have the exact same cards, but they're in a completely different arrangement relative to each other. How does the story change with this new arrangement? How would your interpretation of this reading differ from the first one? Which cards have become more prominent, and which ones look less significant in the new layout? What is the new sequence of events given by this reading? What information has gone from public to hidden, or vice versa?

This exercise is a great way to see how the same cards can provide radically different readings based on how they are laid out relative to each other. Feel free to reshuffle a second or third time to see other potential variations offered by these nine cards. Then, record all of your readings in your tarot journal, along with your thoughts about how the card positions affected your interpretations in each case.

Narrative Spread

This is a slightly more elaborate spread, designed to help you identify all the key components of the story your reading is trying to tell.

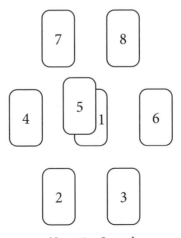

Narrative Spread

In the center of your reading space, lay down one card to represent the central conflict of your reading. This is the MacGuffin, the thing that all the other cards in your reading are responding to. It grounds the rest of the reading, and every other card you pull will be interpreted with reference to this central card. Beneath that, lay out two more cards; these represent the major forces at play. They could be people, institutions, events, personal desires, or external circumstances, but whatever they are, they drive the conflict. The interaction of these two forces creates the tension we see in the central card.

Next, lay out three cards in a horizontal line so that the central card overlaps your conflict card. These cards are a straightforward linear narrative of your past, present, and future. They show you what happened in the past, what's going on now, and what's coming down the pipeline. Remember, the goal is to interpret these not as three separate events, but as a unified whole: three cards that tell one story. The common thread that unites them is the central conflict card, which tells you what that story is about.

Finally, in the space above the past/present/future axis, deal out two more cards. These represent the way forward. They are potential solutions or tools that are available to resolve the conflict at the heart of the reading. These cards offer action and tell you what can be done to fix the problems identified in the rest of the spread.

Taken all together, this spread can provide a complete story, from beginning to end, showing who the relevant characters are, what they do, and why.

Identifying Characters

One of the easiest ways to see who's doing what in a tarot reading is to look at who the characters are in the cards themselves. The cards are a visual storytelling medium, and the images they depict can give you key insight into the *who* of a reading; they can help you identify the people involved in a situation. In particular, they can tell you who is doing what.

Tarot illustrators make careful, deliberate choices while designing their decks. One such choice has to do with the people they put in their cards. Illustrators often reuse models for multiple cards, so the figure in the Six of Swords might reappear as the High Priestess, or the people on the Lovers card might look the same as the people on the Devil card. These connections are meaningful; they are the illustrator's way of indicating to you that these cards are thematically connected. Take note of these similarities, particularly when you are reading.

If a particular character recurs in multiple cards in your reading, that may be an indicator that this character represents a particular person in your life whose actions affect your situation. Sometimes this character is identifiable by physical traits; if the drawing physically resembles someone you know, that may be enough to identify their role in the reading. There have been countless times I've been in a reading, turned over a card, and had someone exclaim, "That looks just like my boyfriend!" Other times, you may need to think about the role or theme signified by the cards in order to identify the person those cards represent. For example, if you perform a reading and you see the same figure appear in the Two of Swords and Eight of Pentacles, you might infer that you're dealing with a person who's currently in the process of learning something new and making a difficult decision. This description could then help you figure out who, exactly, the reading is pointing to.

There is a particular set of cards in the deck that often represent individual people: the court cards in each suit of the Minor Arcana. We'll have the opportunity to discuss the courts in greater depth in chapter 15, but for now, it's worth understanding that each court card has a particular personality. For example, the Queen of Wands is charming, charismatic, and creative; the Knight of Pentacles is diligent and hardworking; the Page of Cups is intuitive and poetic. When these cards appear in a reading, they often identify individuals who share those same personality traits.

The people represented by the court cards may resemble them physically, but they don't need to. In particular, the court cards are usually depicted with particular genders (Kings are drawn as men; Queens are drawn as women), but those genders need not limit our interpretive scope. Any court card can represent a person of any gender—man, woman, or nonbinary. What matters most is the personality signified by the cards, not the gender.

Moreover, the same person can be represented by different court cards across readings. We all adjust our behavior to our circumstances; someone may be shy and awkward in one situation, but bold and domineering in another. The court cards each represent facets of human personality, and people may express new facets when faced with new situations. A court card in a reading, then, tells you how a person is behaving *in the situation relevant to that reading*; it does not necessarily tell you who they are in all aspects of their life. This means that when you do readings about various topics, or about the same topic in various circumstances, the same person may be represented by completely different cards as different aspects of their personality are brought to the fore. Be careful not to fall into the trap of "Person X is always the Knight of Cups." People are more complicated than that, and harder to pin down.

Practice Reading: Who Is My Love?

A young woman comes to you for a reading. She's had a long dry spell in her love life, and she's tired and frustrated with being single. She wants to know when a man will come into her life and what he will be like. Do a reading for her using any spread you like. Take care to use the techniques from the "Identifying Characters" section to help describe the man whom your querent can expect to meet. Record your reading in your tarot journal.

Changing the Story

When you do a tarot reading, particularly a predictive reading, you are telling a story about events that may not have happened yet. This raises an important question, and one that everyone in tarot has to wrestle with: is the future set in stone? If you do a reading that says XYZ is going to happen, is it ever possible to change that outcome so that ABC happens instead? This is a critically important concern. If you give someone a reading and the forecast is grim, you don't just want to tell them, "The future is bleak and there's nothing you can do about it." You want to help them exercise some agency to change the bad outcome into a good one. After all, what's the point of peeking into the future if we can't then use that information to make our lives better?

Tarot readers all have their own views on this subject—and those views are, naturally, informed by their opinions about how tarot works—but the consensus in the tarot community is that a reading does *not* predict an inevitable future that comes crashing down on us whether we like it or not. The future depends on us and our choices. A tarot reading gives a forecast of how things are likely to turn out, based on our actions and our circumstances at the time of the reading. If we change either our actions or our circumstances, then the outcome is liable to change as well. A tarot reading doesn't tell us,

"This is what *must* happen," but rather, "This is what's going to happen if you keep going in the direction you're headed now." If you don't like the outcome, you can always change your direction.

Remember, when you give a tarot reading, you're telling a story, and good stories are character driven. Events in our lives don't just happen to us while we sit passively and accept our fate. We react to our circumstances and take action, and our actions have consequences that, in turn, shape our future circumstances. Part of your role as a reader is to encourage the agency of the people you read for, to show them how they are active participants in the story you tell. Don't just leave a reading at "You're going to get the job" or "This relationship isn't going to work out." Instead, try to delve deeper and use tarot to expose the root causes of these events.

Why are these things going to happen? *How* do they depend on the choices being made, both by your querent and by people in their environment? And what kind of control does you querent have over the situation? We can't control everything in our lives, it's true; other people make decisions that we can't control, and sometimes things just happen—accidents and earthquakes and unforeseeable cases of *force majeure*. Nonetheless, we always have a choice in how we react to the things that do happen. As a tarot reader, you show people where their choices lie and what those choices might lead to. You can help people understand which things they do and don't control (and how to take advantage of the former). When you give someone a tarot reading, you are effectively telling your querent, "Here's the story that your life is telling right now. And if you don't like that story, here's what you can do to tell another one instead."

The Suit of Cups

The suit of Cups deals with emotional connections, both to ourselves and to each other. It governs all relationships, ranging from family to romance to friendship. Just as our emotions are subject to flux and change, the Cups are subtle and complicated, ranging from joy and love to grief and dissatisfaction. The suit of Cups is inherently subjective and personal, dealing with what we *feel*. Although we're often taught to prize objectivity over subjectivity and to treat feeling as a bad thing, the fact of the matter is that emotion is an inescapable, fundamental part of what it is to be human. These are the cards that express that experience.

Ace of Cups

In the Ace of Cups, our cup literally runneth over. We see a hand holding a golden chalice overflowing with water. The Ace of Cups is a card of joy, abundance, and fullness. It is the wellspring of the heart from which all our emotions flow. Here, we find the distilled essence of the suit of Cups: the human heart. All our capacity for love, compassion, and joy is contained in the Ace of Cups, and this card offers an invitation to connect more deeply to our emotional lives. The Ace of Cups asks us to get in touch with our feelings, to be vulnerable, open, and sincere.

The Ace of Cups is an overwhelmingly positive card. As the root of the suit of Cups, this tells us something crucially important about the picture tarot gives us of human psychology: our default emotional state—the essence of our inner lives—is a feeling of love, safety, and joy. That's not to say that we don't have negative emotions, because of course we do. Sorrow, anger, jealousy, and fear are all part of the range of human emotional experience. However, the Ace of Cups tells us that these are not the core experiences of human life. They are not the emotions that define us; rather, they are the emotions we experience when something is wrong and our lives are out of balance. When everything is put right and we are given room to be authentically ourselves, the true nature of the Ace of Cups shines through, and we experience the unbridled happiness that this card often represents.

If something is imbalanced in your life, the Ace of Cups may appear in order to signify that your emotions are at the root of the problem—that there is some inner wound that needs to be healed. In these circumstances, the Ace can represent the negative emotions that overwhelm you, but the goal is always to help return you to a place of joy and peace. Like the Holy Grail, the Ace of Cups is a symbol of harmony and well-being. It is a beacon of hope and a promise that no matter how hard things are now, they can and will get better. Sometimes, when we're really struggling, that promise can seem distant and disingenuous. In those times, the Ace of Cups is something to strive toward. It's a reason to keep moving forward even on your dark days. It is the hope that no matter how hard today might have been, tomorrow can be better.

The Ace of Cups reminds us of the things that really matter in life. We want to love and be loved. We want to be happy, kind, and secure. If we can accomplish that much, then we have lived well. This card shows us the emotional ideals by which to live our lives, the things to strive for and hope for. It shows us, on an inner emotional level, what makes life worth living.

Two of Cups

The Two of Cups is the card in the tarot deck that most represents love and partnership. In this card, we see two lovers reaching out to each other, each offering the other a cup as a show of love and affection. The duality of the Twos combines with the emotional theme of the Cups to make this card all about companionship and love.

Importantly, the love expressed by the Two of Cups need not be strictly romantic. Close friendships, sibling relationships, and even business partnerships can be seen in this card. The important thing here is a reciprocal exchange of affection, a partnership between individuals who support and nourish each other. The relationship depicted in the Two of Cups is an equal one; each person contributes to the other in due measure. It is not a case of unilateral giving or a flowing-forth of affection from one person without any hope for requital. Rather, it is a *shared* love and devotion.

At its worst, the Two of Cups can represent the dark side of romantic love: loneliness, codependency, or possessiveness. These are the things that happen when this card is out of balance. Looking at this card, we see that both figures are standing on their own two feet, firmly planted on the ground. They're each capable of holding their own as individuals, and each offers the other something that enriches them, but neither of them is defined by their relationship. Love can be intoxicating, and it can sometimes overtake and overwhelm us, but the Two of Cups flourishes when it represents two people sharing themselves with each other rather than losing themselves in each other.

Outside of romantic contexts, the Two of Cups signals us to look at our interpersonal relationships and consider the way they affect the situation at hand. Who are we in partnership with? What do we get from other people, and what do we give to them? The suit of Cups emphasizes that our emotional lives depend on our connections to other people, and different cards explore those connections in different ways; the Two of Cups, in particular, focuses on one-on-one relationships. Think not about the larger network of people you know, but about how you relate to each person as an individual.

Partnership can mean many things, and although the primary meaning of this card is connected to romantic love, it would be a mistake to think that the Two of Cups always and only means romance. Rather, it picks out the deep, intimate connections that we experience with other people in any of the infinite ways that humans feel and express their love for each other. The Two of Cups shows us love in many forms, but its core message is always one of devotion and mutual affection.

Three of Cups

The Three of Cups is a card of exuberant celebration. In tarot, the Threes are dynamic cards where things are moving and changing. This energy comes into the emotional suit of Cups as a party—a cause to kick your heels off, let your hair down, and just have fun. We see three women gathered around each other, toasting to some special occasion. The Three of Cups takes us away from the seriousness of life and reminds us that it's okay to enjoy ourselves and to do things with our friends and family just for the sake of celebration. Not only is it okay, it's necessary; as the saying goes, all work and no play makes Jack a dull boy. Other cards in the deck encourage us to work; the Three of Cups, on the other hand, encourages us to play.

Unfortunately, life can't be all party all the time. When we throw ourselves too much into Dionysian revelry, we can sometimes lose sight of our ordinary lives and responsibilities. This is the negative side of the Three of Cups, a caution about intemperance and excess. Everyone needs to have fun and let loose from time to time, but if letting loose is all you ever do, you'll soon find yourself unmoored and directionless, like a college student who needs to stop going to frat parties every night and instead go to class and study.

As a further expansion from the energy of the Two of Cups, the Three can sometimes represent nontraditional relationship structures, polyamory, or (on the negative side of things) infidelity—bringing additional people into the two-person dynamic we saw previously. This is a secondary meaning of the card, which might show up alongside or instead of the broader interpretation about celebration and partying, but it's worth keeping an eye on, particularly in readings that deal with questions of love.

For the most part, though, the Three of Cups points to festive occasions. Birthdays, holidays, weddings—any excuse for people to gather and have a good time in each other's company. The focus of this card is not so much on the celebration itself as on the social connection that it forges. Parties help us be close to people; they help us feel loved and welcomed in our communities. That feeling of love is the common theme that runs through all of the Cups, manifesting in different ways. In the Two of Cups, it was the love we gain from partnership. In the Three, it's the warm, happy feeling we get from a good night out with friends, whether that means dancing in a nightclub or playing board games in someone's living room. The most important part of this card is not what you do to celebrate, but the feeling of togetherness that comes from doing it.

Four of Cups

The Four of Cups is an unhappy card. The energy of the Fours is staunch, static, and unmoving—Fours in tarot represent stability and foundation. When this impassivity is combined with the free-flowing, watery energy of the suit of Cups, the result is rather a muddy, stagnant mess. The Four of Cups is a card of dissatisfaction, malaise, and boredom. It expresses the feeling that nothing's happening even though something should be. In the Four of Cups, we yearn for growth, change, and newness, but instead we find ourselves faced with more of the same, and we are inevitably disappointed.

The image of this card depicts a figure sitting under a tree, scowling at three cups laid out before them. Behind them, a hand reaches out of a cloud, proffering a fourth cup, but our figure is too distracted by their unhappiness with the spread in front of them to notice this new opportunity. Here, we get a visual cue for an important message: sometimes we are so caught up in the things we're unhappy with that we find ourselves unable to notice the new, good things that are coming our way.

Cards in the suit of Cups deal with how we feel, but our feelings are not always aligned with reality. Just because we feel boxed in and stagnant doesn't actually mean that our lives aren't going anywhere. Rather, it means that our perceptions and emotions have been built around a particular narrative, wherein we are passive and stuck. It is often in our power—and indeed, our responsibility—to change that narrative. The ennui of the Four of Cups is self-imposed: the figure in this card is pouting and feeling sorry for themselves rather than taking action to change a situation they don't like. When this card appears in a reading, it often serves as an indication that you are doing the same.

In this sense, the Four of Cups is a call to action. If you don't like your situation, get up and *do* something about it; don't just sit around whining and wishing things were better. The action required may be a material change, such as leaving a job you're unhappy with or initiating a difficult conversation where you feel your voice will not be heard. It may also be a simple change of attitude. Sometimes things are a lot better than we realize, and the Four of Cups directs us to appreciate what we already have. Other times, the change we seek may come in the form of outside help. Just as a hand reaches out to the figure in this card, sometimes the monotony of the Four of Cups is best broken by reaching out to others for support, guidance, and assistance. If you're unhappy and you can't see your way out of it, find someone who can show you the path forward.

Five of Cups

This is another difficult card with a very similar theme to the Four of Cups. Here, we see a figure cloaked in black, looking down at three cups that have been knocked over. Wine is spilling out of them. Behind the figure are two more cups, full and upright, but she doesn't notice them. She is too consumed with how upset she is over the cups that have already spilled.

The Five of Cups is about grief over the things we've lost. We've all had long, tearful nights where we remembered the things we used to have, the people we used to know, or the way our life used to be, and the Five of Cups is the tarot card that deals with those complex emotions of grief, loss, and regret. The woman in this card is totally wrapped up in her loss of the three spilled cups—an emotional state that is further indicated by the way she has literally wrapped herself up in her cloak. In this card, we see the ways that grief can be all-consuming, and though all we see are the spilled cups, we get the sense that this woman is weeping over a much more profound loss. The Five of Cups signals all of the complex, protracted, intense emotions that accompany the awareness that we've lost something or someone and the wish that we could have them back.

However, wishing for something doesn't make it so. We can no more undo our losses than the figure in this card can magically un-spill her cups. That's not to say that we shouldn't grieve when we experience loss; grief is a natural and healthy thing to feel. We have no choice but to experience the emotions signified by the Five of Cups from time to time because loss is an inevitable part of life. Nevertheless, the Five of Cups cautions us about the danger of letting loss overtake us so completely that we become unable to feel anything else. We can and should mourn deeply and sincerely, but if that mourning becomes so intense or so long-lasting that it keeps us from living our lives, it's a problem. The woman in this card is so consumed by sorrow that she neglects her two upright cups entirely; she is so focused on what she has lost that she forgets about what she still has. This is the cautionary tale of the Five of Cups, and it's what we want to avoid.

Grief is healthy. It's our way of honoring what we had. But we must also learn how to let go. The Five of Cups shows us an urge to hold on to the past and to cling to regret over the things we no longer have, but it also reminds us that life does go on, and we do have to keep living. We may feel heartache for the cups we've spilled, but we must not let that heartache keep us from tending to the full cups that are still left to us.

Six of Cups

The Six of Cups, like the Five, deals with the past, but in a much brighter and more wholesome light. We see two children playing in this card, surrounded by cups filled with blossoming flowers. The Six of Cups is about the wonder and magic of youth, the way the world looks through the eyes of a child. It's about play, friendship, and innocence, all tinged with a sort of sweet nostalgia as we look back on these things and remember our past selves. In this card, we learn to see the world through a child's eyes once again, recapturing a glimmer of the bright-eyed curiosity that defines childhood.

In a reading, the Six of Cups may signify nostalgia, literal children, or a figure from your past. It may also represent a more complex relationship to the past, something that you thought was behind you but that is now making a reappearance. This card reconnects us to who we used to be, and usually that's accompanied by a feeling of wistfulness and pleasant remembrance. The reflective mentality of the Six of Cups comes with a rose-tinted memory of the "good old days"—when we think about the past, we often imagine a world where the colors were brighter, the tastes were sweeter, and our problems were simpler and easier to solve. Nostalgia is a powerful thing, and it can change our perception of the present as well as the past. One thing to watch out for in the Six of Cups, then, is this divergence of perception of reality. Just because we remember things a certain way doesn't mean they actually were that way, and we'd do well not to let nostalgia cloud our heads or drag us back into relationships or patterns of behavior that are best left behind.

Not all memories are pleasant, and the underside of the Six of Cups is that sometimes the past comes back to haunt us. If we have unfinished business or a problem that we never resolved, the Six of Cups may suggest that the time has come to face our past issues and finally put them to bed. More often than not, the Six of Cups represents youthful hope and idealism, but sometimes it can show the more upsetting ways the past clings to us.

On the whole, this is a card of looking back at where we've been and realizing how far we've come. It can mean seeing the world through a child's eyes once again, reconnecting with someone or something from our past, or rediscovering something we had forgotten. As all the Cups cards deal with our emotional lives, the Six of Cups particularly invites us to consider the emotional impact that the past has upon us. This card isn't just about what happened in the past, but about how the past makes us feel today.

Seven of Cups

One theme that we've seen emerging throughout the suit of Cups is that perception and reality can sometimes diverge. How we feel about a situation is not always a reliable indicator of what's actually going on. No card expresses this duality more perfectly than the Seven of Cups, which deals with themes of illusion, desire, and fantasy. In this card, we see a man confronted with a vision: seven golden cups, each filled with something wondrous that he desires. From his perspective, he gets to choose between all of these treasures—but in fact, they are an illusion, nothing more than a mirage appearing in the clouds.

At its best, the Seven of Cups expresses an irrepressible creative power. It allows us to see things that aren't there, to imagine the way the world could be instead of how it actually is. This is a much-needed skill in all areas of life, whether you're writing a novel or petitioning for political change. This card shows us the power of dreaming and imagination.

However, at times our imaginations can get the better of us. We wake from a nightmare convinced that there's a monster hiding in the closet; we fantasize about the perfect lover and forget that our romantic prospects are complex people with their own flaws. It can be easy to mistake imagination for reality, and if the energy of the Seven of Cups goes unchecked, imagination can bleed over into delusion. One key theme of this card is the temptation of fantasy—the impulse to spin out an imaginary narrative that suits the way we *want* things to be rather than the way they *are*.

Sometimes we want something so badly that we convince ourselves we can have it, regardless of whether we actually can. We tell ourselves stories, daydreaming about the things we desire. When the daydream becomes strong enough, we can forget that it's just a fantasy and, instead, become convinced of its reality. In such times, we live not in the real world, but in the world as we wish it to be. The problem is, we can't live in a fantasy world forever. Eventually, reality comes crashing in, whether we like it or not.

We all have dreams and wishes, and that's a good thing! Those dreams can motivate us and bring us closer to our goals. The things we wish for, desire, and imagine all reflect on the lives we currently live, and show us the way forward to changing our lives for the better. The important thing with the Seven of Cups is to harness the creative power of imagination and direct it productively, so it helps to enrich our lives rather than serving as an escapist fiction that prevents us from living fully. Let the things you want guide you toward action rather than keeping you suspended in idle fantasy.

Eight of Cups

The core energy of the suit of Cups is about love, joy, and fulfillment, but there are a variety of ways that we achieve that feeling. Sometimes, it comes from reaching out to the people and things that make us happy. Other times, it's about letting go of the people and things that make us *unhappy*. The Eight of Cups is the latter sort of card. This card is about saying "enough is enough" and walking away from a situation that no longer serves you. It signals that the time has come for something to end, and that you need to take it upon yourself to know when to walk away.

In the card itself, we see a cloaked figure with their back turned to the viewer, retreating deeper into the frame of the image and climbing up a mountain into the distance. We don't know exactly what they're walking away from, but one thing is abundantly clear: this person is *done*. They have had enough, and they are ready to walk away and never look back.

Learning when to let go can be a challenging lesson. Many of us have been conditioned to feel like quitting or giving up is a sign of weakness and that we should stick with any project, relationship, or commitment no matter how much grief it brings us. Sometimes, though, there really is nothing to be gained from trying to stay in a situation that makes us unhappy. Having that realization is not a weakness; rather, it takes tremendous strength. Only once we have let go of the things that make us unhappy can we move forward and make our lives better. We have to release the bad things in our lives in order to make room for the good things.

Depending on temperament, some people can err too far in the other direction, dropping every project as soon as it gets hard, abandoning every relationship at the first fight, and failing to follow through on anything. This is, of course, not ideal either. We should only walk away from the things that are genuinely no longer good for us—not the things that challenge us to grow and learn. The Eight of Cups can, in some circumstances, suggest that you're *too* ready to walk away, and that the lesson you need to learn is how to stay rather than how to leave.

In all cases, the theme of this card is about judging whether or not it's time for you to be done with something—and knowing whether you should stick it out or call it quits. This can apply to romantic relationships, work situations, or really any situation in which you have an option to walk away. Often, the decision signaled by the Eight of Cups is a hard one, because it's never easy to consider abandoning something that you've invested your time and energy into. Even so, the Eight of Cups reminds us that it's important to know when enough is enough and when it's time to move on to other, better things.

Nine of Cups

After dealing with some heavier emotional themes in the preceding cards, we finally come back to a card that represents the best aspects of the suit of Cups. The Nine of Cups is often called the "wish" card, because it's the card where you get everything you wanted. In this card, we see a happy man surrounded by full cups, with a smile lighting up his face. The Nine of Cups is about mirth, joy, and fulfillment. It is, like the Ace of Cups, one of the most unabashedly positive cards in the deck.

Nines in tarot are cards of fulfillment. If we understand each suit as a cycle that begins with the Ace and concludes with the Ten, the Nine is the point where we're almost at the peak. The energy of the suit is coalescing, and is almost—but not quite—in its final form. In the Nine of Pentacles, we

saw the material rewards of our labor; in the Nine of Swords, we saw the culmination of our doubts and anxieties. In the Nine of Cups, we see our emotional lives brought to fruition, and we find the feelings of satisfaction and
contentment that come after completing the emotional journey represented
by the other cards in the suit.

This is the card that tells us, "Everything is okay." If you're in the middle of a
stressful time and you're overburdened with problems, the Nine of Cups reassures you that things can—and will—turn out all right in the end. There may
be some bumps along the road, but ultimately, life is good. Just as some cards
in the tarot deck remind us that bad things happen and can't be avoided, the
Nine of Cups reminds us that good things happen too. The dice can roll in
your favor, your plans can turn out the way you'd hoped, and you can get the
things you dreamed of. This is the card where that all happens.

The Nine of Cups encourages us to celebrate the good things in our lives.
It's a card of gratitude. Take a look at your life and consider all the things
that make you feel happy and fulfilled. These are the essence of the Nine of
Cups—a card that invites you, more than anything else, to *let things be good*.
Allow yourself to enjoy your life and be happy. Even if there are some things
that aren't perfect, if there are problems and worries, take the time to set
those aside and focus on the things you do have that make life worth living.
The Nine of Cups reassures you that at the end of the day, everything is okay.
You are okay. You just have to allow yourself to experience what being okay
feels like. For some of us, it can be hard to give ourselves permission to be
happy, but the Nine of Cups promises that happiness is possible for everyone.

Ten of Cups

At last, we come to the end of the suit of Cups. Just as the Ace of Cups was an outpouring of emotion, its culmination at the end of the suit is the Ten of Cups, which represents the shared emotional bonds that tie us to our community. The Ten represents not only the one-on-one partnerships we saw in the Two of Cups, but a much larger, more interdependent network of human relationships. It's about all of the relationships we have, everyone in our lives whom we love and who loves us: family, friends, lovers, and so on. The Ten of Cups is a card of connection, community, and sharing your life with others. In a reading, it points you toward your community and asks you to consider the way that your loved ones connect to the situation you've asked about.

In this card, we see a family dancing under a rainbow. The family here is representative not only of a nuclear family structure—of parents, children, and siblings—but of family in the extended sense. The Ten of Cups is about family not in the genetic sense of people to whom you're biologically related, but rather about the family that you choose: the people you love and trust most in the world. The family represented by the Ten of Cups is the set of people with whom you choose to share your life, in all its good and bad moments. It's the people with whom you celebrate when things are good, and the people who comfort you when things are bad. And perhaps most importantly, it's the people for whom you do the same. The love represented by the Ten of Cups is, much like the Two of Cups, built on a deep reciprocity, and it's about being there for other people just as much as having people who are there for you.

We saw in the Ace of Cups that the essence of this suit is an outpouring of joy and love. In the worldview of tarot, this is what we strive toward in our emotional lives. With the Ten of Cups, we finally reach that, and we learn a profound lesson: joy and love, properly felt, must be shared. The fullness of the suit of Cups is not something we experience on our own or in isolation; it is by necessity something that we experience in relation to the other people who make our lives feel complete. Though the Nine of Cups saw us happy and satisfied, having everything we had wished for, the true fruition of the Cups is in the Ten. Once we have experienced the mirth and gratitude expressed by the Nine, our next step is inexorably to share that joy with the people we love. This is the most important lesson from the suit of Cups, and it is the thing toward which all of the Cups have been guiding us.

PART IV

ASPIRATIONAL

What to Do When You're Wrong

It happens to everyone. It will happen to you over the course of your tenure as a tarot reader, if it hasn't happened already. You will get a reading wrong. You'll tell someone, "Yes, you're going to get the job," and then they will *not* get the job in question. You'll say, "The root of this problem is an honest miscommunication" when in fact the root of the problem is a deep-seated enmity that can't be resolved. You will get things verifiably, embarrassingly wrong.

Part of this is simply a matter of inexperience. When you're first starting out with any new skill, you're bound to make mistakes until you learn how to do it well, and tarot is no different. Right now, you're still getting used to reading the cards, memorizing what all seventy-eight cards mean, and learning how to identify your intuition. That's a lot to deal with, and it's totally okay to be unsure of yourself and to make mistakes as you learn. When you read for other people, be up-front about the fact that you're still learning, and ask them for feedback throughout the reading (as well as after the fact, when the situation they asked about has been resolved). That way, you can both alleviate the pressure on yourself and turn those readings into valuable learning experiences.

However, it is also crucially important to stress that even the most skilled and experienced tarot readers make mistakes from time to time. *Nobody bats a thousand!* All of us have made gaffes in reading, where we said one thing and the reality turned out to be something else altogether, and no matter how good you get at tarot, you will never stop making mistakes.

Humility Is Key

It's okay to make mistakes when reading tarot. It's human. Remember, tarot is an interpretive process. It necessarily depends on the subjective point of view of the reader and the person receiving the reading. It is fundamentally, inescapably personal, and the fact of the matter is, people make mistakes. We're limited and flawed, and we misjudge things all the time. This isn't just a problem with divination; in our day-to-day lives, there are plenty of times when we think we know something and turn out to be wrong, or when we make a decision that we think is for the best, only to later realize that we would have been better off going another direction. In all areas of our lives, we try our best and we get things right a lot of the time, but we can't help screwing up as well. Why should reading tarot be any different?

Understand that this is not a failing of the tarot cards themselves, but rather a natural and forgivable shortcoming in us as readers. Tarot gives us more information than we might otherwise have had and offers a glimpse into the unknown, but having more information does not magically make you—or anyone—perfect at interpreting it. There can be, and will be, times where you misinterpret something or fail to see what the cards are really pointing at. Don't beat yourself up for occasionally getting things wrong.

It's important to realize that being a good tarot reader does not mean you have to predict every detail with perfect accuracy in 100 percent of the readings you give. People often come into tarot with unrealistic expectations, thinking that tarot cards will give them perfect insight into every situation. In fact, being a good tarot reader simply means that the people you read for walk away better informed than when they came to you. If you can reliably give someone additional information and help them gain insight into their situation so that they can make intelligent, informed decisions, then you have done your job.

"Reliably" here doesn't mean a 100 percent success rate; not even the National Weather Service gets their predictions right 100 percent of the time. Rather, it means that you're aiming for your readings to be accurate and informative at a higher rate than you'd get just with educated guesswork.

If you can get your readings right most of the time, and point out themes, events, or people you wouldn't have identified without the aid of the cards, then you're using tarot perfectly well. Being a good tarot reader simply means that on the whole, your querents are more informed with your readings than they would have been without them. Omniscience is in no way a part of the job description.

Every Mistake Is a Learning Opportunity

When you get things wrong, it's important not to bury your head in the sand and pretend that your mistake never happened. Rather, it's best to look back at your reading, dissect it, and figure out why you misinterpreted the cards. Doing so is not about making yourself feel bad for having messed up; on the contrary, it's an opportunity for you to learn from your past mistakes so that you can do better in the future. Every mistake you make in tarot reading is an opportunity for you to learn how to interpret the cards in a more nuanced and accurate way, and for you to explore card meanings that you didn't previously see.

This is part of why keeping a tarot journal is so important. You want to have a record of the readings you've done—of both your successes and your failures. Keeping track of your successes will help you build confidence in your reading skills. When you make mistakes (as you inevitably will), it's easy to get down on yourself and feel like you're no good at tarot, but one of the best ways to combat that feeling is to look over your accurate readings and remember that you actually do have a history of success. The more you read tarot, the more you give yourself the opportunity to establish a track record of successful readings, and having that track record is the best way to build your confidence as a reader.

Conversely, looking at your failures is the best way to improve. By analyzing the things you got wrong in a reading, you can start to see patterns and indications of ways you can improve as a reader. Like a professional athlete rewatching footage from a losing game, you're aiming to identify weak points in your technique so that you can focus your attention on strengthening them. You might notice that there's a particular card you always interpret the same way—for example, you might have a habit of always interpreting the Two of Cups to mean romantic love. Looking back at past readings, you begin to see that there were circumstances where the Two of Cups signified something other than romance, and your narrow view of this card restricted your interpretations and resulted in inaccurate readings in those circumstances. Doing this kind of critical evaluation would then show you that you're in a bit of an interpretive rut with the Two of Cups and need to expand your understanding of that particular card.

Likewise, looking back at past readings can enable you to identify card patterns that may reemerge in the future. Let's suppose you had a past reading where a querent asked you if they were going to get a job they'd applied for. You did a three-card Past/Present/Future spread, and drew the following:

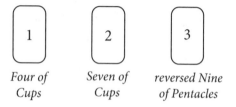

Four of   Seven of   reversed Nine
Cups   Cups   of Pentacles

Unsure of how to interpret these cards, but seeing the reversed Nine of Pentacles in the "future" position of the spread, you told your querent that they would *not* get the job. A few months later, they came back to you and told you that they did get hired at that company, but that the position had been misrepresented to them during the job application process, and the job they were doing was almost nothing like the position they'd thought they were applying for. Looking back on this spread, you can now clearly see the influence of the Seven of Cups on this reading. It introduces an element of illusion and deception, so the reversed Nine of Pentacles didn't mean "Your hard work in this application won't pay off," but rather "Your work will pay off, but you won't get what you thought you'd signed up for."

Why is this information useful? After all, hindsight is 20/20, and it's *much* easier to interpret a tarot reading after you already know the answer to the question. The thing to remember, though, is that you can apply what you've learned here in any future reading you do. Now, if you have another querent who asks you a similar question and you see the Seven of Cups appear in *that* reading, you'll have a sense of what it's doing there and of how it might influence the other cards. Every reading that you do gives you a contextual framework in which to understand the cards you pull in the future.

Practice Reading: A Reading in Review

Look back through your tarot journal and find a past reading where you misinterpreted the cards. Reread your journal entry, then turn to a blank page and begin a new entry. Copy all of the key information about this reading: the question asked, the spread you used (if any), the cards you pulled, how you interpreted each card, and what your overall takeaway from the reading was. If you made a prediction, what did you predict? If you used the spread to aid in decision-making, which course of action did you advise?

Now, underneath all of this information, write down how the reading *actually* turned out. What happened, and how did it differ from your prediction? What information did your reading not inform you about? What did you miss? Try to be as specific and concrete as possible in evaluating what the reading got wrong—not just "The reading said I'd get a boyfriend and I'm still single," but "The reading said I'd get a boyfriend, but all I've had were four dead-end first dates, a one-night stand, and my ex trying to get back together with me." You can write this information out as a set of bullet points or as a freehand journaling exercise, depending on what's most comfortable for you.

Once you've taken note of the things you got wrong about your reading, reach for your tarot deck. Pull out the same cards you drew in your original reading and lay them out in front of you in the same arrangement. Now, knowing what actually happened, interpret the reading again. With hindsight to guide you, how would you read these cards? Write out your new interpretation for the reading. Make sure that you're actually drawing on the meanings of the cards to make this interpretation; don't just say "XYZ will happen" because you know that's how it turns out. You should be making a point to connect the events you *know* with the themes that emerge out of the cards you drew. The purpose of this exercise is for you to discover the relationship between the cards you drew and the actual course of events.

Finally, we conclude with the most important step of this exercise: finding a lesson for the future. The point of looking over your past readings is not simply to come up with a *post hoc* explanation of what they meant. You want to learn from your past mistakes so that you can see what the cards are really saying in future readings.

Write down up to three lessons you can learn from your reinterpreted reading. What are the things you feel you should keep in mind in the future in order to avoid repeating the mistakes from this reading? These lessons could include observations about the way you interpreted an individual card, but they could also include bigger-picture commentary on the way you approach readings. For example, you might have a past reading where you really wanted a particular outcome, and your hopes clouded your judgment when you tried to read the cards. If you know this sort of cognitive bias has been a challenge for you in the past, then it's helpful to pay closer attention to it in the future and ask yourself, *Am I reading what the cards say, or am I reading what I want them to say?*

These takeaways are the most important part of looking back through your old readings. As you continue to read, make mistakes, and learn from them, you may want to keep an up-to-date list of the lessons you're working through. It's easy to develop habits in reading tarot—some of which are helpful, and some of which are not. By keeping an eye on the lessons you've learned from past mistakes, you can help break yourself of the bad habits and improve your reading style as you move forward.

When You Don't Know What to Say

Related to the problem of getting a reading wrong, there is another universal challenge in tarot reading. Every now and then, you ask a question, pull the cards... and then have absolutely no idea what the cards are trying to say. This is especially common for readers who are just starting out and haven't yet grown comfortable with the cards, but even the most seasoned readers will occasionally be stumped. Often, this happens when you draw cards that don't obviously connect to the question at hand—you asked about your love life and drew the Six of Pentacles, or you asked about the logistics of arranging a funeral and drew the Three of Cups. Every reader has had the experience of drawing the cards, feeling their mind go blank, and thinking, *I don't have the faintest clue what this means.*

Thankfully, there are ways to deal with this situation! It's easy to panic in a case like this, but the more you panic, the harder it is for you to see what's going on in the cards. The goal, then, is to shut down that negative feedback loop and make you feel comfortable and collected enough that you can interpret the cards.

Just Start Talking

This is the biggest one. Start by saying *something* about the cards. It can be anything. All you're trying to do is break the ice. Describe the images you see in the cards, or name each card individually and state the keyword or theme you associate with it. Point out how many cards you have from each suit, how many cards are upright or reversed, or any cards that have similar or overlapping themes. Find the cards that make sense to you and are easiest to interpret, and start with those. Just *get yourself talking*. The first thing you say in a tarot reading is often the most difficult; after you've said something—anything—it's easier to find the next thing to say, and the next thing after that. Start talking, and don't let yourself stop talking until you've worked your way through the whole reading.

If you're reading for yourself rather than for a second party, it's still helpful to talk out loud—or at the very least, to write your interpretation down. Doing so forces you to get your mind moving, and it allows your thoughts to flow more freely.

Admit When You're Unsure

Once again, it's helpful to remember that tarot readers aren't supposed to be omniscient. You're only human, and it's okay to be unsure of yourself sometimes. If you're giving a reading and the cards that come up don't make any sense to you, you're allowed to say, "At first glance, I'm not entirely sure what this is saying, but let's work through it." Take the pressure off yourself. You're not an all-knowing, question-answering genie, and you'll get farther by being honest than by trying to bluff your way through.

Consider Other Questions

Sometimes when the cards don't obviously connect to the question your querent asked, it's because they're pointing at a related issue that affects the central question. If someone asks about their family life and they get a reading full of Pentacles, that may be an indication that their work life is overtaking their attention and impeding their ability to spend time with their family. When you get cards that don't look like they're addressing the question you originally asked, consider refocusing the reading on the themes the cards *do* address: "You asked about X, but the cards are saying that in order to understand what's going on with X, we need to stop and talk about Y first."

Solicit Querent Feedback

Tarot reading is a dynamic process. It's an interplay between the cards, the reader, and the querent. If you're seeing themes in the cards that don't make sense to you, remember that you're only one part of the equation. It may well be the case that your querent will be able to help explain how those themes connect to their situation. Talk about the things you're seeing in the reading, then ask the querent if any of those things resonate with them or fit into the context of the question they asked. Your querent knows more about their situation than you do, and they can help you understand how the cards fit what's going on in their life.

Tactfully pressing for more information is an acquired skill, especially because people are often reluctant to speak openly about private and sensitive matters. Sometimes people will hold information back from you or even deliberately lie to make themselves look better, to "test" your psychic prowess, or just because they're uncomfortable sharing. Even so, it's perfectly appropriate for you as a tarot reader to say, "This reading really seems to hinge on XYZ, but you haven't mentioned anything of that sort. Is there something like this going on?" It's then up to your querent to decide how open they want to be and how much information they want to give you. You can't force them to talk to you, but you can give them the opportunity to work with you in order to make their reading more accurate and informative. Often, querents are delighted to help you connect the dots and give contextual information that sheds a clarifying light on your reading.

11

Tarot Ethics

When someone comes to you for a tarot reading, they are placing a great deal of trust in you. Often, querents are discussing the most intimate concerns in their lives: their aspirations, their doubts, their secrets, or the secrets they fear others are keeping from them. I've had querents confide in me about infidelity, domestic violence, bankruptcy, and a whole range of other subjects of immense gravity. People call a tarot reader when they're feeling vulnerable and looking for answers to difficult questions. The nature of a tarot reading requires people to open up and share parts of themselves that they may not be used to sharing—especially with someone who might otherwise be a total stranger.

This vulnerability means that you, as a tarot reader, have an obligation to treat your querents with a high standard of responsibility, honesty, and respect. Ethics are an important consideration in any vocation, but they are even more salient in a situation where someone is placing such a high degree of trust in you. Even if you do not read professionally and only offer readings for friends and family, it's a good idea to consider the boundaries that guide your readings. How can someone expect you to comport yourself when they get a reading from you? How do you expect them to behave? What are the circumstances in which you will (and will not) read for someone?

Some tarot readers have a formalized code of ethics written up in a document that they make available to their potential querents. Others will simply take a moment before any reading to talk over expectations and boundaries. Different people will have different boundaries, and the purpose of this chapter is not to prescribe one official set of rules for ethical tarot. Rather, I'd like to extend an invitation for you to reflect on various ethical issues that might arise in the course of your time reading tarot and to think about where you stand on them.

Honesty and Objectivity

This is the simplest and most obvious ethical principle in tarot, and yet it bears stating explicitly: as a tarot reader, your job is to tell your querents what the cards actually say. This sounds easy, but keep in mind that people will be coming to you for advice in all sorts of situations—and in some of those situations, you're going to have to say things that people won't want to hear. A commitment to honesty in a tarot reading often means telling people no when all they want to hear is yes, or saying, "This looks like a bad idea" to something they're enthusiastic about. Everyone comes into a tarot reading hoping for good news, but the news isn't always good, and unfortunately, you're the one who has to deliver it.

Being an honest tarot reader means being willing to share hard and uncomfortable truths. You don't have to be a jerk about it; there's a way to be honest without being cruel. But your job is to interpret the cards as they fall. That means that if someone asks, "Am I going to get into my first-choice college?" and you draw the Three of Swords and the reversed Eight of Pentacles, *that's* the message you have to deliver. You don't get to lie about what the cards say or do the reading over.

Relatedly, at times, you will have strong personal opinions about what your querents ought (or ought not) to do. If you believe that infidelity is categorically wrong and you find yourself giving a tarot reading to a woman who is cheating on her spouse, it may prove difficult to separate what *you* believe she should do from what the cards are saying. If she asks, "What's the outcome if I continue on my current path?" and you pull the Ten of Cups, your responsibility is to interpret the Ten of Cups. It would be wrong for you to reshuffle and pull a different card in the hopes that it'll align more with your personal opinion.

This touches on another important aspect of tarot reading: impartiality. It's okay to have an opinion, but querents aren't coming to you for your opinion. They're coming to hear what the cards say. You will encounter querents you dislike or who are doing things you don't condone, but if you choose to read for these people, it's important to put your personal feelings aside and read with professionalism. This means withholding judgment on your querents' actions and allowing them to express themselves openly without being sanctioned—even if they're talking about things you find unconscionable.

Everyone has lines in the sand, and if there are things that you cannot suspend judgment about, that's okay. But then the appropriate thing to do is to stop the reading, return a client's money, and say, "I'm sorry, I'm not able to read about this for you. Let me recommend someone who can." Every querent deserves a judgment-free space in which to receive a reading; it's crucial to make a distinction between "This is what I think" and "This is what the cards say." If you can't offer them that, that's perfectly understandable, but then they would probably be better served with another reader.

Money

Not everyone charges money for tarot readings, and that's perfectly okay! But regardless of whether you do or don't charge for your services, it's important for everyone to know what the expectations are surrounding money. If you charge for tarot readings, make sure you tell your client in advance—and agree upon the fee before you start shuffling the cards. The last thing you want is to give a reading where you think you're getting paid and your client thinks it's *pro bono*.

There are a number of different ways to organize a fee structure for a tarot reading. Some people charge per card, others charge for an allotted portion of time, and still others will simply have a flat rate. Regardless of what works best for you, it's good practice to be clear about how much someone can expect to pay. Moreover, make sure that any additional costs are explicit and up-front. If you offer half-hour readings, but there's a surcharge for clients who go over their agreed time slot, make a point to tell your clients about the charge before the reading begins.

You'll find that if you charge for tarot readings, many people you know— including people whom you don't know terribly well—will come to you to ask for a "friends and family" discount, or even for free readings. Likewise, potential clients may inquire about discounts of all sorts: for veterans, senior citizens, party bookings, and so on. Whether you provide such discounts is entirely up to you, and if you choose not to, don't let anyone make you feel bad about it. There's no one right answer here; it's really a matter of establishing and maintaining the boundaries that are right for you. Whatever your policy is, though, you'll save yourself a lot of trouble if you give the matter some thought in advance.

Confidentiality

People will share secrets with you when they come to you for tarot readings. Not always, of course; some readings are about things people discuss publicly. But other times, the subject of a tarot reading will be delicate and personal. It might be something completely secret ("I'm living a double life and I have a second family in Tampa"), or it might just be private ("My wife and I are having trouble in the bedroom"). Either way, when people share personal details with you, there is an implicit demand for trust; they don't necessarily want you blabbing the intimate details of their personal lives all over town. In short, there's an expectation of confidentiality between reader and querent.

It's important, however, to think carefully about what confidentiality means and whether there are circumstances in which a querent's right to confidentiality might be waived. Some examples might include:

- If a crime has been committed or is about to be committed.
- If you fear your querent is a danger to themselves or others.
- If you are called to testify in a court of law.

Or, consider a more personal conundrum. Are you able to make an offer of confidentiality to querents whom you know personally? Suppose that you do a reading for your brother's spouse and find out that they have grossly mismanaged their household finances and sunk thousands of dollars into debt, but your brother doesn't know. Is it wrong of you to keep that secret? Is your loyalty to your brother more important than the privileged relationship between tarot reader and querent?

Moral dilemmas like this are complicated, and different people will feel differently about what sort of behavior is required of them in these circumstances. That's perfectly okay. Wherever your moral compass points you, it's your right to follow that direction. It is important, however, to be clear about your boundaries up front (a refrain that is hopefully starting to sound familiar by this point in the chapter). Before a potential querent ever starts to tell you what's on their mind, make sure they understand what kind of confidentiality they can—or can't—expect from you. That way, they have the ability to decide for themselves whether they feel comfortable sharing private and potentially compromising information.

Legal Restrictions

Pay attention to legal considerations that might affect your reading practice. In some jurisdictions, professional fortune-telling is illegal; this doesn't necessarily mean that you're unable to charge money for tarot readings in those jurisdictions, but it does place important limitations on the kind of claims you can make in promoting yourself or soliciting clients. Whatever the laws in your jurisdiction are, stay abreast of them and make sure that your tarot practice—professional or otherwise—isn't going to get you in hot water. Likewise, be very careful to avoid giving unlicensed medical, legal, or financial advice; all three of these disciplines are carefully regulated, and you can get in serious legal trouble for the unlicensed practice of medicine or law. If someone comes to you and asks for a tarot reading to tell them whether they have cancer, refer them to an oncologist.

Practice Reading: A Court Case

A potential client comes to you for a reading, introducing themselves as Morgan. Morgan explains to you that they are involved in a legal dispute; their ex has filed suit against them in small claims court for violation of a custody agreement. Morgan did, in fact, knowingly violate the custody agreement, but Morgan is hoping that the litigation will proceed in their favor because their ex has a history of frivolous lawsuits. They've come to you in the hope that you can give them a reading to predict how the case will go in court.

Take some time to think about how you would respond to Morgan. Would you perform the reading they ask for? Would you turn them away altogether—and if so, what explanation would you provide for your refusal to read? If Morgan's request makes you uncomfortable on ethical grounds, is there some kind of a middle ground you'd be comfortable with, where you could still give Morgan a reading about a related topic? Record your thoughts in your tarot journal. If you would be willing to read for Morgan, either with their original question or with a modified inquiry, perform that reading and record it in your journal as well.

Querents

Ethics boils down to how we treat people, and the people in question here are, of course, the querents for whom you read. Some of the guiding principles for behavior toward querents are obvious. Treat people with respect and professionalism, and don't be a jerk. Follow those guidelines, and you've got most of your bases covered. However, there are also a few more specific points about the kinds of querents you may get, and they merit closer examination and thought.

Anti-Discrimination

Obviously, "don't discriminate" is a solid foundational principle for an ethical practice in any vocation, not just tarot. Some readers choose to make this principle explicit by sharing an official anti-discrimination policy with their clients. Such a policy serves to reassure clients that the reader will not discriminate against them on the basis of race, sex, gender identity or expression, sexual orientation, religion, country of origin, age, or any of a variety of other protected categories. You may feel that having such an explicit policy is unnecessary for you, particularly if you read primarily for friends and family, but if you are looking to build a professional reading practice, something along these lines can help put your potential clients at ease and establish a professional and inclusive reading environment.

Minors

Are you comfortable reading for querents under the age of legal majority? People have a variety of opinions about this. Some refuse to read for minors under any circumstances, while others have no compunction about it. Still others seek some kind of a middle ground—reading for minors only with the consent of a parent or guardian, or only with an adult in the room. You're fine with whatever approach makes you most comfortable, but it's an important boundary to think about, one way or another.

Querents Under the Influence

Are you willing to read for clients under the influence of drugs or alcohol? This question is even thornier if you charge money for your readings. Ideally, you want to be reading for someone who is coming to you out of their own clear judgment, and because drugs and alcohol can impair judgment, they blur that ethical line. If someone is so intoxicated that they won't be able to remember what you've told them, then there may not be much point in performing a reading, as they won't walk away better informed than when they came to you. And if money has changed hands … Well, it's potentially sketchy, to say the least.

This doesn't mean you can never read for someone in an inebriated state. Rather, it means that you should think judiciously to discern when someone is too inebriated for a tarot reading to be appropriate. If you read at parties or corporate events, you'll often have clients who've had a drink or two; that's a far cry from someone being so drunk that they can't walk straight. It's up to you to determine where you feel the line is.

Querents in Emergencies

Sometimes querents will come to you because their circumstances are dire and they don't know where else to go. You may encounter querents who are dealing with domestic violence, suicidal ideation, financial ruin, medical emergencies, or any of a variety of other extremely urgent and delicate situations. This puts you in a compromising position as a reader; unless you are trained as a crisis counselor, you are likely not prepared to deal with these emergencies. That's not a negative reflection on you! Rather, it's an acknowledgment of just how serious these situations are, and how important it is for people to get help from qualified professionals who are experienced in crisis counseling.

If someone comes to you with an emergency and you feel like you're in over your head, don't read for them. Even well-meaning advice can have life-threatening consequences, and you're better off not giving any advice at all than giving advice that does more harm than good.

However, this does *not* mean you should just turn people away when they're dealing with an emergency! On the contrary: Sit down with someone, listen to them, and help direct them toward resources that *can* help them. When people are feeling desperate and trapped, it can be a huge relief just to have someone to talk to and to feel like they're being heard. Moreover, and more importantly, you can give people the support and encouragement they might need to reach out to qualified professional resources who can help them through their problems. If someone has come to you and asked for a reading, they're already looking for help; point them in the right direction and show them the people who are going to be able to help them best.

It's useful to keep a list of resources on hand for situations like this so that you know where to refer people in crisis. A few important resources in the United States:

- National Suicide Prevention Lifeline: 800-273-8255
- National Sexual Assault Hotline: 800-656-4673
- National Alliance on Mental Illness HelpLine: 800-950-6264
- National Domestic Violence Hotline: 800-799-7233
- For any medical emergency, dial 911

Additionally, you may want to keep contact information for a therapist, lawyer, and financial adviser on hand so that you can recommend their services to querents who might need them. It's natural to want to help people in crisis, but sometimes the best thing you can do to help them is not to give them a tarot reading, but to direct them to qualified professionals whose job it is to deal with those crises.

Third-Party Readings

People request tarot readings when they want more information about things affecting their lives, and one of those things is consistently the influence of other people. Many querents will ask for third-party readings—that is to say, readings about the lives of people other than themselves. Because this is such a frequent request, and because it is one that sits in an ethical gray area, it's worth taking some time to think about now.

Are you comfortable performing a tarot reading and telling your querent about the life of someone who's not in the room, hasn't consented to the reading, and can't speak for themselves? If someone comes to you not for a reading about *his* life, but about his brother's, would you agree to perform the reading? Some readers see no problem with this—after all, the purpose of the cards is to give us information about the world around us, and other people are part of that world. Other readers, however, see third-party readings as inappropriate and an invasion of other people's privacy. Third-party readings are a frequent request, and you'll also get into gray areas with readings that are about a third party but that touch directly on your querent's life, things like "Is my spouse cheating on me?"

As with other ethical questions, there isn't a clear right or wrong answer here. It's a matter of finding the boundaries that are most appropriate for you and that make you comfortable as a reader, then communicating those boundaries clearly to anyone who solicits your services.

12

The Suit of Wands

We come at last to the fiery suit of Wands, the fourth and final suit of the Minor Arcana. The element of fire deals with willpower, passion, ambition, and conflict—anything, in short, that gets our blood boiling. In the suit of Wands, we find the things we strive for. This means external goals, plans, and desires, but also internal ones, as the Wands can represent transformation into the person you wish to be. The Wands span the whole range of things that people aspire to and desire, from lofty ideals like art and spirituality to more animalistic impulses like libido or anger. No matter what, the themes associated with the Wands are burning and intense.

Ace of Wands

If the suit of Wands is fire, the Ace is the spark that gets it to light. The Ace of Wands is an awakening and a beginning—whether sexual, spiritual, artistic, or otherwise. As with the other Aces, it signifies that something new is coming into your life, and in this case, the new thing is directly tied with your wants and ambitions. Maybe you've just now realized what it is that you actually want, and now that you know, you're prepared to set about pursuing your goals. Maybe you're setting a new goal or exploring your creative side with a new medium. All of these things belong to the Ace of Wands.

The image of this card is a disembodied hand reaching out of a cloud, grasping a rod at its base. This imagery is inescapably phallic, and we would be remiss not to note that sexuality is one of the key themes not only of the

Wands in general, but of this card in particular. Remember, tarot encompasses the whole range of human experience, and for many of us, sexuality is part of that experience. The sexual symbolism of the Ace of Wands is not there to be lewd or crass; rather, it's an acknowledgment of the important role that sexuality can play in our lives and the way that it can influence the situations we ask about in tarot readings.

The Ace of Wands is not *only* sexual. At its heart, this card is about new desire and about discovering what it is that you really want. That desire can be sexual, but it can just as easily be career ambition, a desire for self-expression and independence, a new hobby or special interest, or something else entirely. The object of desire is not the focus of this card; rather, the Ace of Wands is about the act of desiring in itself. All of the Aces are about beginnings and potential, and all of them can also see that potential foreshortened and frustrated. In some circumstances, the Ace of Wands might represent repressed desires and the things that you don't allow yourself to want, either because you think you don't deserve them or you don't believe you can achieve them. In cases like this, the Ace of Wands invites you to get in touch with your wants and needs and to try to understand what it is that you really want (and why).

Desire can be a frightening thing—it's intense and all-consuming, and it can be unbearable to want something and then fail to achieve it. However, desire is also the first step to fulfillment. You can never achieve what you want if you don't admit that you want it in the first place, and there is power to be found in claiming ownership of your wants and deciding to pursue them. The Ace of Wands is about that power, as well as the freedom and growth that come with it.

Two of Wands

Once we've decided what we want, we have to figure out how we're going to get it. This is what we see in the Two of Wands: a stage of planning and strategizing, looking at the horizon and charting our course to get where we're going. In this card, we see a man holding a globe and staring off into the distance. He wants the world. Nothing less will satisfy him, and we catch him in a moment of reflection as he tries to figure out how he can attain his (lofty) goal. In the Two of Wands, then, we find our ambitions directed to concrete action. Motivated by the desire of the Ace of Wands, we set ourselves to the task of getting what we want—and the first thing we have to do is make a plan. The Two of Wands asks the question, "Where do I go from here?"

There is a note of caution in the Two of Wands, however. Ambition is not easily satisfied. No matter what we achieve or how far we go, there is a part of us that will always demand more. More success, more power, more money, more accolades, more sex. The man we see in this card is looking to the horizon, but he may find that once he gets there, he's still not satisfied and wants to push even further. He could conquer the whole of the earth and find, at the end of the day, that the world is not enough.

It's also easy to get so caught up in our plans that we forget things don't always—or really *ever*—go perfectly according to plan. You might have an idea of how you're going to get from Point A to Point B, but everyone else around you has plans of their own, and you have no control over their thoughts, desires, and actions. At its best, the Two of Wands shows flexibility in dealing with contingencies and adapting to new situations, as your plans will have to change with changing circumstances. At its worst, this card is rigid and unwilling to deviate from its pre-established plan, even after it's become apparent that the plan won't work.

Remember that the Wands deal not only with desire, but also with will. The Two of Wands unites these themes. It is the application of will to achieve desire by laying out your intentions in a plan of action. In a reading, it suggests that you need to take the time to plan out your next steps. You know where you are and where you want to end up; now, it's just a matter of breaking down the space in between into manageable steps so that you can get closer to your eventual goal. You don't just wake up one morning and magically find that you've achieved everything you wanted. Instead, you have to work at getting the things you want, and the Two of Wands is where you figure out how to do that work in order to get the payoff you're looking for.

Three of Wands

In the Two of Wands, we laid our plans; in the Three of Wands, we see those plans set in motion. This card depicts a man—the same man from the Two—standing on a hilltop overlooking a harbor below, where merchant ships are coming and going from a port. This man is, quite literally, watching his ships come in. He is seeing the first fruits of the plans he's made, as his business begins to grow and his goals begin to take shape. He hasn't yet achieved what he set out to do, but he's reached a point where he can see that he is on his way there.

The Three of Wands is the point where a goal shifts from being an idle fantasy to something more concrete that looks like it can actually be accomplished. It's the tipping point between *wishing* for something and *striving* for it. When you first start to want something, it lives only in your imagination. It's not fully real. Only once you've started to put in the work, and seen the effect your efforts have, does your goal become real. That's the experience of the Three of Wands.

In its more negative aspects, the Three of Wands can represent the other end of the spectrum: frustration in your goals, obstacles and blockages, and seeing your desires dissipate rather than take shape. For those who haven't put in the necessary work, the Three of Wands carries a clear message: simply wanting something doesn't make it so. If you want your desires to be realistic goals, you have to do more than sit around hoping things will work out. You have to *act*. If you rely on the assumption that everything will turn out for the best without doing everything in your power to make it so, your complacency can actually keep you from accomplishing the things you desire.

On the whole, the Three of Wands is a hopeful card. It's the feeling you get when you realize your plans are all coming together. It's the moment when your business venture lands its first big investor, when you schedule a second date with someone you really like, or when you get a call from someone interested in a project you've been pitching for months. The Three of Wands captures the warm, glowing sensation that starts in the center of your chest when you realize, *I just might pull this off.* Keep doing the work, don't let early successes get to your head, and you'll find your goals growing more distinct and more realizable. There's still a long way to go from there to full success, but when the Three of Wands appears in a reading, you can usually see your destination beginning to take shape on the horizon.

Four of Wands

The stable energy of the Fours gives us a respite from the dynamic (but exhausting) themes that dominate the suit of Wands. Up to this point, the cards we've seen in this suit have been about the things we desire and are trying to attain; the Four of Wands shifts our focus and instead invites us to show gratitude for the things we already have. This is a reflective, introspective, celebratory card. It's all about recognizing the good things you've got going for you and taking the time to show due appreciation for the people and things that fill your life.

In this card, we see a couple gathered under a makeshift pavilion with an awning woven of greenery stretched above them. They hold bouquets of flowers and their heads are wreathed. In the distance behind them, a castle looms, and we can see other members of a party gathered together. We don't know exactly what it is that they're celebrating, but it's clear that these people have come together for some festive and joyous occasion.

The Four of Wands is associated with all the ways, big and little, that we express gratitude. From writing a thank-you note to celebrating Thanksgiving dinner, the Four of Wands encompasses any action where we take stock of the good things in our lives and go out of our way to show appreciation for them. Extending this symbolism further, the Four of Wands can be indicative of the good things themselves—the reasons we have to be grateful in the first place. If you're facing a situation that feels overwhelming and hopeless but the Four of Wands turns up in your reading, it's a reminder that even in the midst of the greatest strife, there is often some good to hold on to if you know how to look for it.

In addition to the feeling of gratitude and the good things that inspire it, this card often represents a happy occasion of some kind. Weddings, bat and bar mitzvahs, graduation ceremonies, housewarming parties, and retirement all fall under the purview of the Four of Wands. These are occasions where we stop to celebrate a major accomplishment, a rite of passage, or a new and exciting experience in someone's life. In all cases, there's a feeling of joy and contentment that comes from the knowledge that things are *good*. This card is not just about partying for the sake of a party, as we saw in the Three of Cups; rather, it's about celebrating because you have some real cause to do so.

The Four of Wands encourages us to seek out the best things and people around us and to take the time to honor them. The practice of gratitude doesn't make your problems magically disappear, but those problems are easier to deal with when you remember the good in your life.

Fiue of Wands

With the Five of Wands, we shift gears and focus on the more aggressive features of the suit. This card wants to get in a fight! We see five people locked in combat, each carrying a quarterstaff. The Five of Wands is a bellicose, confrontational card. When this card shows up in a reading, there's a conflict ready to blow up in everyone's faces. Tensions are high, communication has broken down, and everyone is ready to throw hands.

We're often taught that conflict is a bad thing, to be avoided at all costs. Sometimes this is true, and it's usually ideal to try to resolve your problems in a nonconfrontational way before resorting to outright argument. However, there is something inescapably honest and efficient about the Five of Wands. This card doesn't mince words or beat about the bush; when the Five of Wands has a problem, it deals with that problem in the most direct way it knows. This can be unsettling if you're a conflict-avoidant person by nature, but conflict is not an inherently bad thing. It allows you to face your problems head-on and deal with them rather than letting them worsen through inaction.

The Five of Wands is a card of strife, to be sure, but it's a healthy kind of strife. This card gets everything out in the open. It lets you air your grievances, forces you to hear the grievances others have against you, and then pits you against each other until you've resolved your problems, one way or another. It's a messy, wearying, and often upsetting process, but it's an effective one. In this sense, the Five of Wands often shows up in the context of sporting events or other competitions, with the attitude of "May the best person win." The spirit of the Five of Wands is conflictual, yes, but it's not encumbered by unfairness, duplicity, or cruelty.

Even healthy conflict can sometimes go too far, and if you find yourself fighting all the time, the Five of Wands has overstepped itself. The goal of this card is to fight in order to clear out sources of strife—not to fight in perpetuity and with no apparent reason. When you're angry or in the midst of a conflict, it's easy to get so caught up in your anger that you forget why you're fighting in the first place. This is, needless to say, far from ideal, and it's an indication that the quarrelsome energy of the Five of Wands needs to be reined in.

In this context, this card warns that conflict cannot and should not be your whole world. As important and healthy as it is to deal with your problems in a direct manner, you should also take care not to declare war at every slight offense, nor to pass over conciliation and leap into unnecessary and unproductive battles. As important as it is to know when a fight is needed, it's just as important to know when it's time for peace, friendship, and resolution.

Six of Wands

The Six of Wands depicts a triumphant parade led by a central figure crowned in laurels. Whether he is a returning war hero, a victorious athlete, or a newly crowned prince, this figure is a striking symbol of victory. The theme of this card, then, is success, victory, and triumph.

In a reading, the message of the Six of Wands is straightforward: accomplishment. This card forecasts success—and even more specifically than that, public recognition for success. With the Six of Wands, we see not only a job well done, but also acknowledgment of that fact by other people. The figure in this card hasn't just triumphed; he's getting a *parade* for it. The Six of Wands places success in the public eye, so doing well and receiving acknowledgment for doing well are inexorably connected.

Success and accolades can go to your head, and the fame connected to the Six of Wands is not always a good thing. It can easily turn into shallowness, vanity, and a dependence on the opinions of others. At its weakest, the Six of Wands can develop into a pathological insecurity and a feeling that your own accomplishments are never enough unless you can get the approval of others. The shadow side of success and recognition is failure and ignominy, and while the Six of Wands rarely signals the latter, our unrealistic expectations can make a moderate success feel like a terrible failure. One of the key lessons of this card is in learning to recognize what true success is and measuring it by internal metrics rather than by the way others perceive us.

With the victory of the Six of Wands, there's also an implicit question: "What comes next?" Remember, the Wands are a suit of striving, of desiring, and the Six of Wands is a pivotal point where you've achieved the object of your desire. Like the winning quarterback at the Super Bowl, you then have to answer the question, "What are you going to do next?" Do you choose to rest on your laurels, satisfied with what you've accomplished? Or do you set your sights on a new, even more ambitious goal and keep pushing for further and higher success?

The accomplishment represented by the Six of Wands can be quite dizzying, as success and recognition are piled upon you. For people who are unaccustomed to being in the spotlight, this can even be an uncomfortable and anxiety-inducing experience. Nevertheless, it is important to realize that this card represents public adulation that has been *earned*. In the Six of Wands, people don't simply celebrate the central figure for no reason; he has earned their respect and praise by his actions. The same applies to you. If you find yourself succeeding and worry that you don't deserve it or haven't earned it, remember that the Six of Wands only awards praise to those who are worthy of it. Your accomplishments may well be greater and more impressive than you have allowed yourself to believe.

Seven of Wands

The Sevens in tarot deal with perspective, in one way or another. As we move into the back half of the suit of Wands, we shift our stance from a proactive to a reactive one. Up to this point, we've been dealing with the things we want to achieve—things we don't yet have. But now, in the Seven of Wands, our attention is redirected toward defending and keeping hold of the things we don't want to lose. The Seven of Wands forces us to reorient ourselves and take a defensive position rather than an offensive position.

This card shows a man backed up against a cliff, facing off against unseen adversaries. We've all been in this position before, feeling cornered and defensive in the face of an attack. This could be a literal attack, perhaps in the form of a threat to your physical safety, but it could just as easily be a situation in which someone is gunning for you at work, your finances are unstable, your friends have proved unreliable, or you're caught up in a legal battle. Whatever the specifics, the Seven of Wands indicates a situation in which you feel *threatened*. Your back is against the wall, you're in a bad situation, and you can't see a clear way out. Moreover, the Seven of Wands often represents a feeling of isolation; the figure in the card has to face his enemies alone, and can't rely on help from anyone else.

The lesson of the Seven of Wands is a hard one, but an important one: the only way out is to persevere. There is no way this man can get down off the cliff, except by fighting his way through the people who stand against him. When you're cornered and vulnerable, it's tempting to give up hope and stop fighting for yourself, but if you do so, you will surely fail. The Seven of Wands pushes you to keep fighting in the face of what looks like an unwinnable struggle—not because there is a guarantee of victory if you do, but rather because there is a guarantee of defeat if you do not.

This card can sometimes represent an unwarranted level of defensiveness. If you allow yourself to fall too much into the mindset of the Seven of Wands, every critique can seem like a personal attack, and every minor annoyance can seem like a life-or-death threat. Like a mother bear who is overly protective of her cubs, it's easy to be too conscious of potential dangers. This attitude can actually be counterproductive, as it drains your energy and leaves you depleted when it comes time for you to confront a legitimate threat. Invest your energy wisely. The vigilant, steadfast, perseverant energy of the Seven of Wands will serve you best if you reserve it for situations where you're actually under attack.

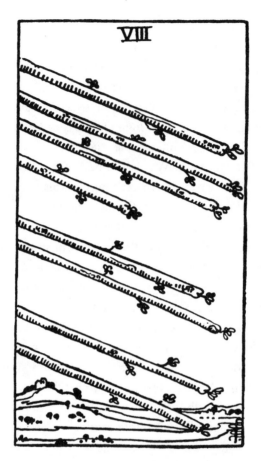

Eight of Wands

Along with the Three of Swords and the Ace of each suit, the Eight of Wands is one of the only cards in the Minor Arcana that do not traditionally feature any human figures. Instead, we see eight rods flying through the air, thrown by some invisible hand. This is a card of motion, energy, and rapid change. In the Eight of Wands, big things are happening, and they're happening so quickly that ordinary people can't keep up—hence, the absence of human representation. This card is about speed and vitality. Whatever's happening, the Eight of Wands indicates that it is happening quickly.

The Eights of the Minor Arcana all connect to themes of freedom and motion, and nowhere is that more apparent than in the Eight of Wands. In a reading, this card may denote travel, physical exercise, or a package in transit.

Conversely, it may express its themes in a more abstract way: as political ascendancy, a career promotion, a sudden new opportunity or step forward, or an ordinarily slow process being expedited. If things are moving and speeding up, in a literal or figurative sense, the Eight of Wands is at work.

The challenge of the Eight of Wands (which will be familiar to us by now from other cards in the suit) is that it can get out of control if it goes unchecked. This is the nature of elemental fire; it burns, keeps burning, and doesn't know when to stop. If you're not careful, a candle flame can burn your house down, and a carelessly discarded cigarette can start a forest fire. With the Eight of Wands, things can speed up *too much*, to the point that they're moving at a breakneck pace and you can't keep up with them or control them. Expansion, growth, and dynamism are all good things, but they can be taken too far. If your career is advancing so fast that you find yourself in a job you're unqualified for, if an athlete is so obsessed with improving that she turns to performance-enhancing drugs, or if an author is so consumed by writing that he forgets to sleep, then the Eight of Wands has gotten out of hand.

This card travels at warp speed. If you know exactly where you're going and you have a clear path ahead of you, that can be a wonderful thing—so long as you take care not to overshoot your target or trip yourself up on the way. The Eight of Wands is at its best when it's given direction, a concrete goal, and a step-by-step plan to get there. Having these things allows you to productively guide the frenzied energy of the Eight of Wands and make sure that it's bringing you somewhere you want to go rather than just taking you for a ride.

Nine of Wands

After the outpouring of energy in the Eight of Wands, it's no surprise that the Nine of Wands is a more sedate card. In fact, the Nine of Wands is downright fatigued. In this card, we see a weary, wounded man with a bandage around his head leaning on a staff for support. Behind him is an array of staves planted into the ground, reminiscent of a military trench. This man is a soldier caught in a war of attrition. He's tired, beaten, and broken. He needs a rest, but the war is ongoing and rest is unavailable to him. The central theme of the Nine of Wands is exhaustion, fatigue, and a desperate need for respite.

The sad truth of the Nine of Wands, however, is that we often don't get a respite when we need one. Sometimes, it's just not an option for us to take a break and lay our heads to rest. When we have responsibilities that need to be tended to—like when there are things that have to get done and we're the only ones who can do them—then we can't rest, no matter how much we might need to. The Nine of Wands tells us to carry on, not by inspiring us and filling us with hope and vigor, but by reminding us that *giving up is not an option*. We keep going simply because we have no other choice.

Perhaps it goes without saying, but this isn't sustainable in the long term. Human beings are not built to last without periodic rest and refreshment, and if you try to carry on indefinitely without giving yourself time to pause and recuperate, you will eventually burn out. The Nine of Wands can serve as a warning that you're heading in that direction. If you see the Nine of Wands in a reading, its message is often, "If you don't stop and rest sometime soon, you're going to collapse from sheer exhaustion." You may be so overburdened with responsibilities that rest is not currently an option, but the Nine of Wands tells you to *make* it an option; make room to give yourself a reprieve, even if it means abandoning some of the things you're currently committed to. Otherwise, the need for reprieve will assert itself whether you like it or not.

When you're so exhausted that you can't see straight and you don't remember what it's like to get a good night's sleep, it can be difficult to remember what restfulness really is and why it's important. If you've gone so long without something, you begin to forget how much you need it. Nevertheless, the Nine of Wands affirms that rest—and even beyond that, leisure and free time—*is* a basic human need. You can't go forever without it. If you're tired in a deep way, the sort of tired that you feel in your bones, you have to pay attention to that and prioritize your needs.

Ten of Wands

We are now at the end of the suit of Wands, and we finish on a somewhat dissonant note. The Ten of Wands is a heavy, oppressive card. In it, we see a figure carrying a bundle of firewood in his arms. He is on his way home and is almost there, but his head is down and his view is obscured by the load he carries, so he can't see where he's going. The Ten of Wands represents being overburdened and overtaxed, trying to carry the weight of the world on your shoulders.

All of the Tens represent the outcome of their respective suits, the consequences of the previous nine cards. In the Wands, where we've spent almost the entire suit striving to attain new things, we find that once we have everything we want, we are then faced with the overwhelming task of managing it all. When we're wrapped up in our desires, it's easy to think we want everything, and when we act on those desires, we sometimes bite off more than we can chew. The Ten of Wands is the moment when we realize what we've done, take stock of the commitments we've made, and try to figure out how to deal with the ways we've overextended ourselves.

The Ten of Wands tells us that we can't do it all. We might wish we could, but the fact of the matter is that there are only so many hours in a day, and we are human beings with limited time and energy. We cannot keep an infinite number of plates spinning in the air. If we try to, we'll inevitably let some of them come crashing to the ground, and we'll let down both ourselves and the people who are relying on us. This card serves as a warning not to spread yourself too thin. Focus on doing fewer things and doing them well rather than trying to do everything and ending up doing it all poorly.

The central character of the Ten of Wands will find his way home eventually, and he will be able to lay down his burden. As overwhelming as the Ten of Wands can be, it doesn't last forever; this card represents a temporary situation that can be fixed, both through hard work and through the careful establishment and maintenance of boundaries. Don't overcommit yourself, work hard on the commitments you already have, and you will be able to lessen your load in the long run. Things will be tough for a while, but if you narrow your focus and apply yourself to the things you have to do, you can succeed. Just take care to learn from the experience, and don't overburden yourself in the same way the next time around.

PART V

PERSONAL

The Importance of Objectivity

Objectivity is a funny word, and it means different things to different people. For some, *objective* is simply synonymous with *true*; an objective statement is one that is true regardless of whether people like it or agree with it. For other people, *objective* means something more like *dispassionate* or *emotionless*, with the implication being that objectivity requires a calm, inhuman, almost robotic attitude. Still other people see objectivity as something procedural, a feature of a process rather than of a person or a statement, as in double-blind medical studies or other scientific experiments.

In chapter 11, we had the opportunity to touch upon the notion of objectivity as it applies to tarot and why it matters for tarot ethics. Here, we'll go into greater depth on the subject, and we'll explore a couple of scenarios when it can be difficult to remain objective as a reader. In short, objectivity in the context of tarot means interpreting what the cards actually say without projecting your own hopes, desires, or expectations onto them. The great enemy of objectivity in this sense is cognitive bias, where you allow your own preconceptions to color your perception and interpretation of the cards in a reading. Broadly speaking, there are two ways cognitive bias can influence your reading: you can see what you *want* to see, or you can see what you *expect* to see.

Consider the following cases. Suppose you go on a date with someone and you really like them. You have a charming time, the conversation flows easily, and you're deeply attracted to them. When you get home after the date, you pull a card just to see whether this is something real—and of course, you're hoping that the answer is an unequivocal "Yes." In this situation, it's hard to put your own wants aside and read the card dispassionately because there is an outcome that you want; some part of you is not actually looking for a tarot reading, but rather just wants to be told, "Yes, this will go the way you hope it will," regardless of whether that's true. This is a mistake that I, personally, have made on more than one occasion. It's all too human to see what you want to see instead of what's actually there.

As a second example, suppose a friend comes to you for a reading. The circumstances are the same—he's just been on a wonderful date and he wants you to draw a card to tell him if this is going to turn into something real. However, in this case you know that your friend is a serial monogamist who has a habit of wanting to get very serious very fast, and you don't trust his judgment when he tells you this was a date like no other. In this case, you're coming into the reading with a preconception about your friend, and that preconception can color the way you interpret the cards you draw. If you expect the message to be something along the lines of "Hold your horses, you're getting way ahead of yourself," then there's a good chance you'll see that message in the cards even if they're actually signaling something totally different.

Cognitive bias is a normal, human, and inescapable part of tarot reading. It comes part and parcel with tarot, precisely because tarot is an inherently subjective and interpretive process. You don't have to eliminate your own biases completely in order to be a good tarot reader, but you do want to be conscious of them and do what you can to countermand them. Be honest with yourself and with your querent about what you want to see in the reading and what you expect to see in the reading, and then try to read past those biases and see what else there is to be said about the cards. Look for the things in the reading that you didn't expect and don't necessarily want to see; more often than not, those are the signposts that point you toward what the reading actually has to say.

Practice Reading: Evaluating Your Bias

Do a reading for yourself on a subject you care about—something where there's a potential outcome you *really* want. The goal of this exercise is to become aware of your own cognitive bias and the way it can affect your reading, so the stronger your desire, the more productive the exercise will be.

Lay out your cards, then do a first-pass interpretation of them where you say exactly what you were hoping to see. Interpret all the cards in the most charitable way possible; twist and hack at their meanings as much as you need to in order to make them fit what you want them to say. Give yourself the ideal tarot reading and tell yourself everything that you were hoping the reading would say. Interpret the cards fulfilling your wildest fantasy, where everything goes your way. Record this interpretation in your tarot journal, but don't put the cards away when you're done.

Walk away from the reading for a while to clear your head. Make yourself a cup of coffee, watch a movie, go for a walk around the block, or occupy yourself in some other way. Do something to get your mind off the reading and its contents. When you feel you've been away long enough and can look at the cards with fresh eyes, return to your reading.

Now, interpret the cards again—but this time, in the most pessimistic way possible. Crush your dreams. Deliver the cruelest, bleakest, most hopeless interpretation you can possibly come up with, telling you that you won't get anything you're hoping for and the whole situation is going to turn out for the worst. Just as you did with the positive interpretation of this reading, you should feel free to twist the meanings of the cards at this stage of the exercise. Be a little disingenuous in your interpretation if you have to, but find a way for every card to tell you you're going to fail. Record this interpretation in your tarot journal; then, leaving the cards where they are, walk away and clear your head again.

Come back a third and final time to interpret the cards, and this time, try to be honest. Deliver the most accurate, sincere reading you can, focusing not on what you want the cards to say (or on what you're afraid they might say), but on what they actually mean. This third interpretation requires a great deal of honesty and introspection on your part, as it forces you to set aside your personal feelings on the matter; if you find yourself getting too close to the first-pass interpretation, try to stop and correct your course. Record this reading in your tarot journal, and take particular note of the ways it deviates from your first two interpretations. What are the things you saw in your third reading that you didn't see the first or second time around? What are the things you highlighted in the earlier interpretations but that you left by the wayside when you were trying to be honest and objective about the cards? Paying attention to these things can help attune you to your own biases, and it can make it easier to recognize and account for those biases in future readings.

Reading for Yourself

It's hardest to avoid cognitive bias when you have some personal stake in the subject you're reading about. For this reason, reading for total strangers can actually be easier than reading for yourself or even for close friends and family. When you're pulling cards for somebody you don't know personally, you have less of an investment in pleasing them and telling them what they want to hear. It's easier to be impartial and to look only at what the cards say because you don't care as strongly about the outcome as you would if you were reading about your own issues. Likewise, you don't have a loaded set of preconceptions and expectations about a total stranger, so it's easier to filter out your own opinion and just read the cards.

Reading for yourself is a massive challenge, and many readers choose not to do so precisely because it's so difficult to be objective. We're all only human; we can't help wanting to put a thumb on the scale to make a reading look more positive than it is. There's a sort of magical thinking at work here, the subconscious notion that if you can doctor a tarot reading and make it say the thing you want, then the real world will follow suit. We often can't help feeling that tarot *creates* the future and that by forcing a reading to tell us what we want to hear, we make it actually happen. This is a perfectly understandable impulse, but unfortunately, that's not how the world—or tarot—works. In fact, all tarot does is describe the world, not influence it. If you don't like the prediction that tarot gives you, the best thing you can do is to listen to it honestly and try to understand why the outcome is what it is. That way, you can take concrete steps toward changing your actions and redirecting your course.

When you're considering reading tarot cards for yourself, you have to maintain an exceptional and unflinching level of self-honesty. This starts even before you shuffle the cards, with the question, "Can I really read objectively about this?" Are you in a state of mind where you'd be willing and able to discern an unwelcome message in the cards? If not, there's no shame in that. At some point in their career, every tarot reader will encounter a question that's just too close to home, one for which they can't perform an unbiased reading. Being honest with yourself about your limitations will allow you to go to another reader and ask them to do the reading for you, ensuring that you get a *bona fide*, impartial assessment of your situation. It's a smart move to ask someone else to be objective when you're not sure that you can.

If you decide that you do want to read for yourself rather than soliciting someone else's services, go right ahead! There's nothing wrong with reading for yourself, and in fact it's a wonderful way to gain experience with the cards. To ensure objectivity and hold yourself accountable in the reading, I recommend recording every reading you do. Write down the question you asked, the cards you drew, and what you thought they meant; then, come back to the reading after a week or two, look over the cards again with fresh eyes, and see if there's something you missed or would interpret differently. This is one reason why a tarot journal is such a valuable learning tool: it allows you to revisit your readings when you're no longer in the heat of the moment so you can ask yourself, *Is that really what the cards said? Or was my judgment clouded?*

Hopes and Fears Spread

This spread is designed to help you disentangle your personal perceptions from the reality of a reading. Start by laying out two cards in the center of your reading space. Below them, place three cards in a row, and above them, place one final card; the final shape should be an upward-pointing triangle.

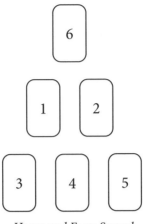

Hopes and Fears Spread

The two cards in the center represent you (or your querent) and the question being asked. The bottom row of the spread represents the subjective perceptions that affect your understanding of this question: from left to right, what you *hope* the answer will be, what you *fear* the answer will be, and what you *expect* the answer will be. Finally, the crowning card at the top of the triangle tells you what the answer to your question actually is. This is a useful spread to use when you're overwhelmed by your personal feelings on a reading and you just want a clear answer. It's designed to help you cut out the noise and see what's really going on.

Rereading for the Same Question

Sometimes people aren't satisfied with the answer a reading gives them (particularly if the answer was one they didn't want to hear). They'll come back to you the next day or the next week, asking the same question as before and insisting you give them a new reading. Like a child who whines "Pleeeeeease?" until his parents give him what he wants, these querents will pester you for another reading—and another—and another—until you tell them what they want to hear.

People often ask for a second reading in the hope that it will contradict and annul the first, but doing so betrays a fundamental lack of trust and respect for tarot as an interpretive discipline. When a reading gives someone an answer, they have to accept that answer—and if they don't like it, they can work to change their actions in order to redirect their path. If they reject the answer they're given and try to reread in the hopes of a different one, they're not engaging with the process of tarot in good faith.

It can be hard to accept the results of tarot readings we don't like. We often compulsively check, double-check, and triple-check information on things we care about. If I'm planning a weekend at the beach and the weather forecast says it's going to be gray and rainy, you can bet your bottom dollar that I'm checking that forecast every two hours. People have the impulse to do the same thing with tarot. Once again, there's an element of magical thinking here: *If I can get the reading to say XYZ will happen, then it will actually be so.*

Unfortunately, doing another reading in a short span of time will not make things clearer or make the outcome more desirable; rather, it will muddy the waters. In my experience, if you ask the same question too many times in too short a span, the cards will sort of shut down, spitting out readings to the effect of, "You got your answer, now why are you still asking?" Trying to get a different answer by asking the question again is not a fruitful endeavor.

The general policy here is that you should only reread for the same question once circumstances have significantly changed, although some readers institute a specific waiting period, such as thirty days. When you do a reading, you give a querent their answer—it's then up to them to act on the information you've given them and wait for their situation to play out. The best thing to do is trust that the cards came up right the first time you drew them, according to whatever mysterious mechanism underlies the function of tarot. Whatever you drew the first time you asked the question, those were the right cards; trust them and go with them until there's significant new information that calls for another reading.

Practice Reading: New Information

Your friend Jamal is a banker who's dissatisfied with his current job. He comes to you for a reading about his career. He wants to see if there are any opportunities for change coming his way. Do a reading for Jamal using the spread of your choice, and record the reading in your tarot journal. Wait two weeks before proceeding with the rest of this exercise.

Two weeks later, Jamal comes back to you to inform you that he's landed interviews for two different positions. The first is a job almost identical to the one he currently has, but at a different bank; he was told about this job opening by his sister-in-law, who works there. The second position, which he found through an online job posting, is as an in-house accountant at a large marketing firm. He'd have to move to a new city for this job, but it pays better than the other position.

Do a second reading for Jamal using the spread of your choice. In particular, pay close attention to anything that parallels your first reading for him. Are there any recurrent cards between the two readings? Are there similar themes emerging? What has changed, and what has stayed the same? Think about how Jamal's circumstances have altered from the time when you gave him his first reading, and how those changes might influence the advice and interpretation you offer in your current reading.

Significator Cards

Some readers like to use a technique known as the *significator card*, which can serve to ground a reading and establish a direct connection to the querent. To use this technique, sort through the deck prior to shuffling and choose one card that you feel represents your querent. Then remove this card from the deck and place it face-up in the center of your reading space. Shuffle the remaining seventy-seven cards and proceed with the rest of your reading as normal. Unlike the other cards in a reading, the significator is not pulled at random; it is preselected by the tarot reader based on its significance and connection to the querent.

Significators are a divisive topic in the tarot world. Some readers love them and use them in every reading. For these readers, a significator helps ground the reading and gives it a central focus. By choosing a card to represent the querent, you orient all the other cards you draw around *them*. You make your querent the literal focal point of the reading, and this can help to focus your interpretation of the cards; it serves as a signal that this reading is about this person, not anybody else. Depending on your view of the way tarot works, that signal may be a message to your own subconscious, or it may be an indication for the forces (personified or otherwise) that make the "right" cards turn up, whether those forces are angelic guides or the general principle of synchronicity. When you use a significator, you are telling your deck that you want the right cards for the question asked by this one particular person.

On the other hand, some readers eschew significator cards altogether. These readers largely feel that a significator doesn't add anything of note to a reading. You've already specified your question by asking it, so why do you need an extra card to focus your reading? Moreover, readers who disfavor significators often dislike them because they skew the randomness of a tarot reading. When you preselect one card and remove it from the deck, the consequence is that this card cannot turn up anywhere in your reading. If your significator is the Queen of Cups and the message from the cards would best have been symbolized with the Queen of Cups in the "future" position of your spread, that can no longer happen. You've limited the expressive power of the tarot deck, albeit in a very small way.

It's worth noting that if you do use a significator, there are still countless other ways that any theme can be expressed in your reading. Working with a seventy-seven-card deck rather than a full seventy-eight will not ruin the reading; it's just that some readers stand on principle and dislike any technique that interferes with the randomness of a tarot draw. As with so many things in tarot, the choice of whether or not to use significators is entirely a matter of personal preference. My advice would be to experiment and try it out for a while to see if you like it. If you try it and decide it's not for you, there's no harm in that, but it's good to test tarot techniques and get a feel for what they're like before you choose one way or another.

Choosing the Significator

There are a variety of ways to choose which card you want to use as a querent's significator, and they range in specificity and depth. The most common practice is to use a court card as a significator, as the courts are the cards that most represent individual human personalities. However, some readers choose not to restrict themselves to the courts, also choosing from the Minor Arcana or the Major Arcana if they feel that one of those cards is more appropriate to the question at hand.

The Fool, Magician, or High Priestess

One classic technique is to use one of the Major Arcana as a significator, depending on the querent's gender. Typically, the Magician card (numbered I in the majors) is used to represent a man, and the High Priestess (numbered II) is used to represent a woman. One disadvantage of this technique is that it relies on a binary notion of gender and doesn't make room for nonbinary or gender-nonconforming querents, but you could easily add to this practice by using the Fool (numbered 0 in the Major Arcana) to represent querents who don't identify as men or women. The Fool is classically an androgynous card and has no particular gender assigned to it, as it represents undifferentiated potential. Thus, it would make an appropriate significator for people who exist outside of the gender binary.

A second disadvantage of this technique is that it lacks specificity; you're not identifying much about your querent beyond their gender. Depending on what you use your significator for, this might be perfectly all right, but some of the other techniques we'll discuss allow you to focus more closely on your querent's personality and situation—rather than the abstract, archetypal representation afforded by using one of the Major Arcana.

By Theme

You may wish to choose a significator that thematically represents the question being asked or the situation that the querent has described. In this case, you have the whole seventy-eight-card deck to choose from. If a querent is asking about their love life, you might choose the Two of Cups; if they're feeling overloaded at work, the Ten of Wands might be appropriate. You could also choose any of the Major Arcana—for example, the Devil would make perfect sense as a way to center a reading about addiction. This is a more unconventional way to use a significator, as it represents the question more than the querent, but it has the advantage of allowing you to get hyper-specific. Of course, the flip side is that whatever card you choose will then not appear in your reading. If you're doing a reading about someone's love life, you might *not* want to choose the Two of Cups as a significator so that you can see whether that card turns up in the course of the reading itself. There's a trade-off.

Courts by Personal Appearance

A simple way to use the court cards as significators is to choose one that visually resembles your querent. This is merely a superficial connection—just because a card looks like your querent doesn't mean that the personality represented by that card is indicative of what your querent is actually like—but it can be remarkably effective. Moreover, it affords your querent an opportunity to literally see themselves in the reading. Most querents aren't familiar with the intricacies of tarot symbolism, but if you show them a card that looks like them and say, "This is you," that's something they'll be able to understand without explanation. You don't have to limit yourself to the court cards if there's a figure elsewhere in the deck who particularly resembles your querent, although the courts are the most commonly used.

At this point, I should offer one major caveat: this technique *only* works if your deck contains representations of people with a variety of physical traits. Many tarot decks, particularly the iconic ones published in the twentieth century, exclusively depict young, thin people of Western European descent. If you have a diverse clientele, you won't be able to use this technique to choose significators for them unless you actively seek out a deck that's more representative (something that I wholeheartedly recommend).

Courts by Rank

Each suit of the Minor Arcana has a court of four cards, which are arranged hierarchically in an order inspired by European feudalism: Page, Knight, Queen, and King. Each of these ranks has certain connotations and associations, which can be matched to the roles that people fill in everyday life. These roles, in turn, can help you choose a significator.

- Pages are messengers, and they are at the bottom of the hierarchy. Someone who is just starting out in something (a new job, a course of study, etc.), who occupies a service role, or who shares information with others can be represented by a Page.
- Knights are adventurers and warriors. People who travel a lot or are enmeshed in a conflict, as well as those who are guided by some higher ideal or aspiration, can be represented by Knights.

- Queens are ostensibly less authoritative than Kings, but they wield a hidden power. Anyone who pulls strings behind the scenes, or who deals with the problems that other people don't know about, can be represented by a Queen.
- Kings are in charge. Bosses, landlords, elected representatives, or anyone in a position of power and authority can be represented by a King.

Kings and Queens also tend to be more mature, while Knights and Pages represent more youthful people. These ranks can be combined with the meanings of the four suits to choose a significator. For example, if you have a querent who has just come out as gay and is struggling with his sexual orientation, you might choose the Page of Wands—someone who is just beginning to discover his sexuality. If you have someone who works as a mortgage loan officer and is asking about his work life, you might choose the King of Pentacles. And so on; you get the idea. Incidentally, understanding the hierarchy of the courts and the roles of each card can also help you interpret the court cards when they appear in a reading.

Courts by Personality

Finally, if you know your querent well enough, you can choose to assign them a significator based on their personality by choosing the court card that most closely matches them in temperament. You could choose the Knight of Cups for a dreamy-eyed idealist, the Queen of Swords for a no-nonsense analytical type, and so on. This requires a certain amount of familiarity with your querent—obviously, it's much harder to identify the personality of someone you've just met. If you can do it, though, choosing a significator in this way establishes a strong personal connection that incontrovertibly centers the reading on your querent. For more information on the specific personalities of the sixteen court cards, see chapter 15.

Practice Reading: Who Am I?

This is a reading to select a significator card for yourself, if there's not already a card that you strongly identify with. Remove the sixteen court cards from your deck and set the rest of the deck aside. Shuffle the court cards and ask, "Who am I?" Then, draw one card. This is your new significator.

Take note of the visual symbols in the card and what they mean to you, as well as the themes associated with the card's suit and rank. Look up the meaning of this card in chapter 15 and take some time to reflect on the key personality traits of this court card. How are you like this card? How are you different? Where do you see your strengths and weaknesses reflected in it? What do you think you could learn from this card?

Record your thoughts in your tarot journal. Use this court card as the significator in readings you do for yourself, at least for the short-term future. People change and grow over time, and you don't need to use the same card as your significator for the rest of your life, but in the short term, you should focus on working with this card and understanding how it represents you.

Recurrent Characters

You'll sometimes find, particularly as you read for yourself, that you come to associate particular cards with individuals in your life. Suppose, for example, that the Queen of Pentacles is the significator you use for your mother. Over time, as the Queen of Pentacles starts to appear in readings, you may see that card and make an automatic connection to her—so that even if your question was not originally about your mother, you interpret the reading as suggesting that she is involved in some way.

This can be a good thing. It's an easy way to make intuitive connections between a reading and specific people, and doing so allows you to be more concrete and detailed in your interpretations. Moreover, it is invariably true that certain people play a large role in your life and are involved in most of the events and issues you care about, so it's unsurprising that those people would recur when you read for yourself. The more involved someone is in your life, the more likely you are to see them appear over and over again in your personal readings. If you're doing a reading, you see the Queen of Pentacles, and your first thought is of your mother, it's worth following that intuitive connection.

However, you should be wary of drawing a one-to-one connection between a person and a card. Remember that each card has a variety of meanings and possible interpretations; you don't want to get caught in a rut of always thinking that card X represents person Y, because then you might miss the possibility that it represents someone (or something) else entirely. This is true of all the cards, not just the courts. Don't fall into the trap of thinking that the Two of Cups always signifies romantic love or the Six of Wands always represents a sporting event. Remember that each card has a great deal of depth and nuance to it, and you're best off if you can open yourself up to the wide range of potential meanings that come with any given card.

This cautionary note extends in the other direction too. It's not just a matter of avoiding "Card X always represents person Y"; you also want to steer clear of "Person Y is only ever represented by card X." People are complicated. They relate to us in a variety of ways, and they perform myriad functions in our lives. You may be used to thinking of your mother as the Queen of Pentacles, but if she's asking you to show her how to use her new computer, she's taking on a role that's much closer to the Page of Swords. Be open to the possibility that the same person can be represented by different cards in different circumstances; otherwise, you'll end up in a reading where you see the Page of Swords and think, "Gosh, this sounds like it's describing my mother, but that can't be right because she's the Queen of Pentacles."

It's a really good thing to start to notice patterns in your readings and to take advantage of recurring cards and themes to streamline the interpretive process. That's a sign that you're getting more familiar, confident, and comfortable with tarot. It's just important not to allow comfort to develop into complacency. Make sure that the patterns you identify are actually serving to enrich your readings (and to make them more accurate) and aren't just a crutch that you lean on to avoid exploring more complex or unfamiliar meanings in the cards.

Practice Reading: Using Your Significator

This is a simple exercise that takes advantage of the significator technique. Shuffle your deck while thinking about a particular issue or situation that you've been dealing with. For this exercise, do *not* remove your significator from the deck; shuffle it in with the rest of the cards. Then, when you feel the deck is adequately mixed, flip it over and look through it, taking care to preserve the order of the cards. Sort through your deck until you find your significator. Pull out your significator, the first card above it, and the first card below it. (If your significator is on the top of the deck, loop back around to the bottom, and vice versa.)

These cards make a simple three-card reading. Your significator, of course, represents you. The card immediately above your significator represents your situation as it stands currently, and the card immediately below your significator represents the outcome of your question. You can also do a variant of this reading and add more information by taking two cards on either side of the significator rather than just one. As always, interpret your reading and then record your interpretation in your tarot journal.

15
The Court Cards

The court cards are unique among all the cards in a tarot deck. Where other cards represent a theme or cluster of closely interrelated themes, the court cards represent personalities. They're people, and because people are messy, so are the court cards. These cards are complex and sometimes self-contradictory. They express individualities, people with their own tangled set of thoughts, desires, and feelings. In a reading, court cards often signify particular people who affect the querent's situation, but they may also symbolize aspects of the querent's own psyche, or even the impersonal characteristics of their circumstances.

Remember as you read these descriptions that all people are complicated and multifaceted. The court cards represent particular personalities, and when the courts stand in for someone in a reading, there likely won't be a perfect one-to-one overlap between the personality of the card and that of the person. You're not looking to identify someone who is exactly like a given court card in all ways, but rather to find prominent personality traits that align with the way your querent or someone in their environment thinks, acts, or feels.

In addition to identifying the personalities represented by the courts, you may also wish to look at their rank and suit. Chapter 14 included some discussion of the different roles and stations of the four ranks in the tarot court; these roles are not only helpful in choosing a significator, but they can also help you to understand the personality and archetypal energy embodied by a particular card. Kings are people who act like they're in charge, regardless of how much power they actually wield, whereas Pages are people for whom every day is a new discovery and who are always trying to learn new things from the people around them. It's worth noting that the court cards can represent people regardless of gender, so you don't need to limit yourself with the assumption that the Queens can only represent women and the Kings can only be men. The focus is on the personalities attributed to the cards, not on their gender.

Moreover, each rank in the tarot court has an elemental correspondence:

- Pages correspond to earth. They are like a seed that has been planted and is waiting to sprout, containing the potential for growth and actualization in their respective suits.
- Knights correspond to air. They are active and constantly in motion, full of ideas and quick to change, processing the energy of their suits in an abstract, idea-oriented way.
- Queens correspond to water. They are intuitive and good at understanding and managing people's feelings. They manifest the energy of their suits passively and receptively.
- Kings correspond to fire. They are dominant and powerful, and they like to be in control; they direct their suits with will, passion, and clarity of purpose.

Understanding these elemental correspondences can give you a fresh layer of insight into each of the court cards. The King of Pentacles brings a fiery personality to the earthy domain of his suit, the Queen of Swords brings watery insight to airy intellectual pursuits, and so on. If you're feeling confused and stuck with the courts, look to their elemental properties and you may well be able to understand them better.

With that note, all that's left is to introduce the cards themselves.

Page of Pentacles

The Page of Pentacles is someone who's going to do big things. As a relentlessly practical person who is good with her hands and willing to work hard in order to achieve her goals, she is a natural cultivator. Here is someone who converts possibility into actuality, who knows how to turn a maybe into a yes. The Page of Pentacles doesn't get lost in wild fantasies or unrealistic dreams; instead, she has her feet planted firmly on the ground. She knows what she wants and that it's achievable, and she's focused on making it happen.

Unfortunately, because of her low rank in the court, the Page of Pentacles doesn't have access to all the resources she might need to realize her goals. She has the work ethic, but she may be short on money or connections, and she'll have to hustle harder than other people in order to find the success she knows she can achieve. She is still very much at the start of her journey, someone who is on track to becoming successful but is not already there. Her primary goal is to foster abundance and growth, not just for herself but also for the people around her.

This Page's strengths include diligence, foresight, and the ability to plan and budget. On the negative side, she may be a bit of a miser, so concerned with pinching pennies that she denies herself even the smallest luxuries; often, this is reflective of a reality in her material circumstances. The Page of Pentacles is someone who knows what it means not to have enough, and who takes great pains to make sure she never experiences that again.

Knight of Pentacles

The Knight of Pentacles is a laborer. He works hard, takes pride in his work, and doesn't complain, even when he's overburdened. He is unfailingly patient and dedicated. The Knight of Pentacles is not a terribly flashy person; he doesn't talk much or draw attention to himself, and he's unlikely to put forward ideas of his own, but if you give him a job to do, he will work at it without complaint until it's done (and done well). He is loyal and disciplined, and his word is as good as a legal contract.

He can, however, be a bit of a stick in the mud. The Knight of Pentacles takes everything seriously, including himself. He has little patience for or interest in humor and play, and he disapproves of people or activities that he perceives as frivolous. He errs toward a high degree of faith in established institutions and authorities. The Knight of Pentacles likes the status quo, feels comfortable in it, and distrusts anything too new or unconventional if it might overturn that status quo. This is someone who likes to take orders and who follows them well; unconventional thinking is not in his wheelhouse.

His sense of loyalty and stability extends beyond the domain of work. In all areas of life, the Knight of Pentacles is reliable but somewhat boring. That's not necessarily a bad thing; dependability is a rare virtue, and we all need someone we can rely on no matter the circumstances. The Knight of Pentacles is that person. When you're in trouble and you need help, he will always be there for you, even if he doesn't make a big show of it.

Queen of Pentacles

The Queen of Pentacles is a warm, nurturing figure who orients herself toward others and takes personal pride in the care she gives to the people in her life. This is the sort of personality you find in doctors, in chefs, and in charity workers: someone who finds satisfaction in being able to take care of others. The Queen of Pentacles is selfless, not as a facade or for social clout, but because she really, genuinely cares and wants to help people.

It is easy, however, for the Queen of Pentacles to give too much of herself. Because she is so oriented toward the needs of others, she may sometimes neglect her own needs in an attempt to provide for the people around her. This tendency toward self-abnegation is an unfortunate trait in the Queen of Pentacles. She really believes, on some intractable gut level, that her role in life is always to minister to others, even at her own expense. She defines herself in relation to others, and it can be difficult for her to acknowledge that her own wants and needs are just as legitimate, and just as important, as those of others. The Queen of Pentacles struggles to understand that she has worth as a person in her own right, independent of what she gives to other people.

On the whole, the Queen of Pentacles is good-natured, generous, and attentive to practical details that other people tend to forget. She likes to solve problems before they even appear, and she rarely solicits praise for her work; thus, her contributions often go unnoticed, and people may not realize just how much they rely on her.

King of Pentacles

Here is someone who appreciates the finer things in life. The King of Pentacles wants the best of everything: the best food, the best wine, the finest clothes, the nicest car, the house on the top of the hill. He's disposed to luxury and financial excess, not because he's showing off, but because he wants the things that are the best. We live in a material world, and the King of Pentacles intends to take full advantage of what it has to offer. He is excellent at managing money and material resources, and he's successful in business; it may sometimes seem like everything he touches turns to gold.

The King of Pentacles is prone to excess in all things, and that can sometimes get him in trouble. He cares a great deal about money and the privilege that comes along with it, and he has a hard time understanding people who don't have or don't want those things. He also has a habit of conflating material needs with emotional, intellectual, or spiritual ones; introspection and reflection don't come easily to him, and he's the type to eat his feelings or pursue retail therapy rather than confront challenges in his inner life.

He thrives in positions of leadership and is excellent at making difficult decisions. The King of Pentacles doesn't mind playing bad cop if he has to; he knows what needs to be done and he sees the best way to do it, even when that's unpopular. For the same reason, he gives excellent advice. He's honest and direct, and he won't pull any punches—so if you're making a big mistake, he will tell you as much to your face.

Page of Swords

The Page of Swords is an inventor, an innovator, and a tinkerer. Fiercely curious and intellectual, she aims to understand the foundational principles of everything in the world around her. She wants to know how things work and why. In this, she is the archetypal scientist, forming hypotheses and testing them, doing experiments to see if her ideas hold up to scrutiny. She questions everything. The Page of Swords is constantly looking to learn and shows a profound curiosity for any subject she encounters.

Her quick wit and talkative disposition make her a great conversational partner, but in her enthusiasm she sometimes talks over people and forgets to include them. Her mind moves at light speed, and for those who don't know her well, it can be difficult to keep up with what she's thinking. She's passionate about intellectual subjects, but she's not great with people; she can be socially awkward and often misses social cues. She doesn't know how to be a shoulder for someone to cry on, and she prefers clean-cut problems with concrete solutions over the complications of human emotional life.

The Page of Swords loves a puzzle and is an extraordinary problem solver. She is uniquely talented at analyzing a situation and getting to its root causes—the sort of person who has a solution for every problem. Her greatest strength is taking abstract ideas and applying them to the concrete world, bringing theory into practice and *doing* something measurable with all of her study and inquiry. The Page of Swords doesn't just study things for the sake of knowledge; she wants to use that knowledge to make the world a better place.

Knight of Swords

The Knight of Swords is lost in his own ideas. In some ways, he's a visionary: He sees the world as it could be, not as it actually is, and his vision is full of fantasy and wonder. He has big ideas and big plans—but unfortunately, he's not very good at following through on them. He's a brilliant thinker, but he is not a practical person. As good as his ideas are, they live in the world of ideas, and he struggles to actualize them and bring them into reality. This is someone who will draw up a blueprint for a house but never build it, someone who will write a thousand-page manifesto about problems with the extant political system but will be unable to provide any concrete proposals for policy reform.

To understand the Knight of Swords, think of the stereotypical image of the absentminded professor. The Knight of Swords is the sort of person who can tell you everything there is to know about the fall of the Roman Empire, but he's also the person who locks his keys in the trunk of his car and who can't find his glasses when they're already on his head.

He is an intellectual, and he can provide invaluable insight on any issue from an abstract point of view, but at the same time, he's a bit of an airhead. He tends to be forgetful and unreliable, neglecting his real-world commitments because he has other things on his mind. The Knight of Swords benefits from structure and external accountability, which can supplement his own lack of discipline and focus, but he also needs the freedom to express himself and think creatively, as is his nature.

Queen of Swords

The Queen of Swords is, like the other members of her court, an analyst. Unlike the Page and Knight, however, her analytical side manifests most strongly as an insight into human nature and behavior. She understands what makes people tick, and she can often evaluate other people's actions with a degree of clarity, objectivity, and discernment that they don't have themselves. The Queen of Swords has a piercing intellect that gets right to the core of people's subconscious feelings and beliefs; her ability to examine those beliefs and apply conscious insight to them is her greatest strength.

Other people may find her insight off-putting; the Queen of Swords values truth above all else, and she refuses to put up with dishonesty and ignorance. She is the sort of person who won't make any claim without thorough research backing it up, who expects others to do the same, and who has little tolerance for empty bluster. If others try to pass themselves off as something they're not, she sees right through the facade. Unfortunately, her insistence on the truth often garners her a reputation for being frigid and contrary. The Queen of Swords sees right through the facades that people try to put up, and oftentimes people don't appreciate having their affectations dismantled.

The Queen of Swords is a natural leader whose no-nonsense approach leads others to trust and respect her, even if grudgingly so. She is a careful person who thinks through everything before she speaks or acts, and because of this she is a good judge of character, an unbiased mediator of disputes, and a reliable partner in any enterprise.

King of Swords

Here we have a master strategist. The King of Swords surveys the world as if it were a chessboard, and he views the people around him as pieces to be moved. He is capable of forming complex plans stretching far into the future, with contingency plans taking a variety of scenarios into account. No matter what comes his way, the King of Swords is prepared. He is cool-headed and good in times of crisis because he's likely already considered what he would do if such a crisis arose. Whatever the circumstances, the King of Swords responds swiftly, decisively, and competently.

His great downfall, however, is that he does not play well with others. The King of Swords trusts his own intellect and the plans that he makes, but he doesn't trust other people to make good decisions. Rather, he thinks that he should be in charge of making everyone else's decisions for them. It's easy for him to fall victim to the idea that everything would run perfectly if only he were in charge. He can be stubborn and uncooperative in any environment that requires teamwork and compromise, and it is difficult to convince him that other people have ideas worth listening to or that someone else has noticed something he hasn't.

Although he chafes at having to work cooperatively or under others, the King of Swords flourishes when he's independent. He has a great deal of foresight and his judgment can generally be trusted, but he keeps his cards close to the chest and may not want to explain himself—if asked to do so, he'll fire back with "Because I said so" and leave it at that.

PAGE of CUPS.

Page of Cups

The Page of Cups is a gentle soul. Sensitive and creative, she expresses herself through music, art, and poetry. She is generally a deeply sincere person who wears her heart on her sleeve and assumes that others do the same; as such, she takes everything to heart. Compliments and praise will send her soaring, but criticism, insults, or meanness will cut to the quick and leave wounds that last for a long time. She can be naive and overly trusting, and as a result it is easy for her to be hurt by worldly types who take advantage of her innocence. The Page of Cups assumes the best in people, and she wants to be liked by everyone; the combination of these two traits makes her particularly vulnerable to peer pressure.

Her manner of expressing herself is unconventional; she has difficulty arranging her thoughts in a linear narrative for other people to follow because she operates more on intuition than on intellect. The Page of Cups *feels* her way through the world, and she's baffled by people who demand cold rationality. To her, life is about the colors of the sunset and the lyrics of her favorite song. If she lives a life that doesn't let her prioritize her artistic nature, she'll feel stifled, stagnant, and oppressed.

The Page of Cups is curious about other people and wants to get to know them. She's a wonderful listener, and she can find empathy with others' experiences even when they're far removed from her own. Kindness and compassion are at the core of who she is, and she lives her life trying to understand people and make herself understood in return.

Knight of Cups

Meet Prince Charming. The Knight of Cups is a romantic, someone who sees the world as full of beauty and enchantment to be shared. He has a dreamy, far-off look in his eyes, and he has such charm that everyone around him can't help but to fawn over him. He falls in love easily (and often), believing every time that his feelings are deeper and realer than anything anyone else has ever felt.

This can get him in trouble, however; he's good at the romance of relationships, at the roses and chocolates and candlelit dinners, but he doesn't like the uncomfortable work of really getting to know someone and building something lasting. The Knight of Cups loves the idea of love, but when the real world doesn't measure up to that idea, he loses interest and moves on to something new. This is true in other areas of his life, not just in relationships. The Knight of Cups is constantly chasing a dream, aspiring to something purer, better, more beautiful—only to find once he has it that its reality is not everything he'd made it out to be.

The Knight of Cups lives in a world of ideals, and he doesn't understand why everything can't be perfect. It's difficult for him to be content with what he has, and instead he is always yearning for a fantasy that's just out of reach. His idealism can be a strength, however. The Knight of Cups refuses to settle for less than he's worth. No matter what his life is like or what the world is like, the Knight of Cups sees how it could be better, and he strives to improve it.

Queen of Cups

The Queen of Cups feels everything. She is overflowing with empathy for other people, and feels their joy—and their sorrow—as if it were her own. This can be an enormous challenge for her, as she has difficulty drawing and maintaining boundaries. It's hard for her to say no to people, even when the request is unreasonable, because she deeply, *deeply* cares. She wants to see things from others' point of view and to help them with their struggles, so it's hard for her to see when someone is being selfish and taking advantage of her. The Queen of Cups' greatest flaw is that she isn't sure where she ends and other people begin.

She is generally rather passive, preferring to listen rather than speak and to observe rather than act. In general, she's a bit of a wallflower, and she doesn't like to be the center of attention. Large crowds overwhelm her because she has to be "on" around other people, and doing so requires a great deal of work.

The Queen of Cups contains hidden depths that most people don't see— because when they look at her, they only see the part of her that reflects themselves. Although she doesn't make a big show of it, she has deeply held passions, and the best way to get to know her is to show a genuine interest in the things close to her heart. Because she so easily mirrors the people around her, it can be difficult to find out what she loves for her own sake, but she appreciates anyone who makes the effort to try and see the real her.

King of Cups

The King of Cups is a peacemaker and a diplomat. Here is someone who understands both sides of any conflict; he situates himself in the middle of conflict so that he can help people's voices be heard. He understands the feelings of others, but he sets himself apart from them, offering sympathy rather than empathy. The King of Cups is a compassionate person, but his compassion is tempered by perspective, and he often feels that the best way to wield it is by not getting directly involved.

He is relentlessly patient, calm, and good-humored, even in the face of someone shouting and insulting him. Like a parent whose child is throwing a temper tantrum, the King of Cups will let people tire themselves out, then will try to connect with them once they're more willing to listen. Sometimes, though, his even comportment can manifest as condescension and paternalism, and he has the habit of treating people like children when he's not pleased with the way they're acting.

The King of Cups makes an excellent counselor, as he has the perspective to help people reflect on their own feelings and actions. Through him, other people are able to consider what they're doing, why they're doing it, and where they may have gone astray. Because the King of Cups holds himself back in his interactions with others, he's good at helping people without his own biases and preconceptions clouding their relationship. However, the unfortunate consequence of this is that he, himself, is difficult to truly know. Still waters run deep, and the King of Cups' placid demeanor often makes it difficult—if not impossible—for people to know him intimately and plumb his depths.

Page of Wands

The Page of Wands is an explorer on the brink of discovery. This is someone who's experiencing something new and exciting for the first time, something that's going to radically change her experience of the world. For the Page of Wands, every day is a new adventure with the promise of excitement and passion. She has a thousand and one interests, and she'll talk about them to anyone who will listen. She likely lacks expertise in these interests—she's a jack of all trades and a master of none—but that doesn't make her passion any less sincere, and she is constantly looking to expand her interests.

As a rule, the Page of Wands is good at starting projects but not so great at finishing them. She can be impulsive and easily distracted, starting something new on a whim and then forgetting about it as soon as something else catches her eye. Most of the time, she is directed by her passions, and as those passions come and go, it can be hard for her to hold on to the motivation to follow through with long-term commitments. Similarly, the Page of Wands is prone to sudden flare-ups of intense, heated emotion: anger, lust, competitiveness, and so on. She doesn't have a great deal of self-control and composure, and she can get lost in the intensity of her experiences.

The Page of Wands is unmatched in energy, vitality, and enthusiasm. She's not the most tactful person in the world, nor the most emotionally mature, but she has an irrepressible sense of joy and wonder. She loves what she does, and she does what she loves—to her, that's what life is all about.

KNIGHT of WANDS.

Knight of Wands

The Knight of Wands is a rebel. Here is someone who needs a cause to fight for, who is never satisfied unless he's pushing against the status quo. Whether that's in the political arena, in the workplace, or elsewhere, the Knight of Wands demands change and innovation for their own sake. He always has to be growing, changing, and moving on to bigger and better things. He gets bored easily, and when he's bored he's inclined to pick a fight just for the excitement of it. Restless and impetuous, the Knight of Wands has a lot of energy and has to direct it *somewhere*; otherwise, he gets sullen and angry, the stereotypical rebel without a cause.

He is at his happiest when he's in motion and doing something that feels positive and productive. The Knight of Wands loves to travel, will take any excuse for an adventure, and never backs down from a challenge. He can be overly competitive at times, but his competitive spirit comes from a love of the struggle that's to be found in healthy competition—not just from a need to win. More than anything else, the Knight of Wands likes to strive, and he has to have a goal that he's working toward. Competition is just another way for him to fill that need.

The Knight of Wands loves everything exciting and unconventional, and he refuses to follow the path that others have chosen for him. He's the king of sex, drugs, and rock 'n' roll. He'll never be satisfied with an ordinary, quiet life—he'd much rather live fast and die young than resign himself to what he sees as a mediocre existence.

Queen of Wands

The Queen of Wands is warm, charming, and charismatic. She has the conversational grace to put anyone and everyone at ease, and she makes friends easily because people feel they can truly be themselves around her. She's a magnetic, intriguing personality, and people find themselves drawn to her for reasons they can't quite explain. The Queen of Wands is great at parties because she has a story for every occasion and knows how to keep her audience enraptured. More than just a good storyteller, she is equally a good listener, and she has the ability to make everyone she speaks to feel as if they are the most interesting person in the world.

Her life is glamorous, and sometimes that can mean it's insubstantial. The Queen of Wands cares a great deal about appearances and reputation, and she may be inclined to prioritize the way things look over the way they actually are. More than anyone else, she understands the importance of making a good impression and the way that people's perceptions can shape reality, so she puts a great deal of care into her public image.

Make no mistake: the Queen of Wands has personal ambitions of her own. She's good with people and generally well-liked, but that's not her only goal. The Queen of Wands believes that in order to get ahead in life, you have to treat people well; thus, she's a master of networking. No one understands the value of human connection better than she does. She knows that her goals are better achieved cooperatively than combatively, and she prefers to win people over to her way of viewing things rather than fighting them to get what she wants.

King of Wands

At long last, we meet the King of Kings himself: the King of Wands. Here is someone who radiates power and authority, who wields it as effortlessly as he breathes. There can be no doubt that the King of Wands is in charge. He does what he pleases because it genuinely doesn't occur to him that he might be beholden to anyone else. When he gives instructions, people follow them; trying to argue with the King of Wands would be as nonsensical as telling the sun not to shine. Even if he doesn't occupy a position of institutionalized authority—a boss, a politician, or something similar—he has an effect on the people around him. He is, simply put, used to getting his way.

However, it would be a gross mischaracterization to reduce the King of Wands to selfishness and power. He is a natural leader who leads by example and inspires others with his own genuine passion and commitment. In everything he does, he gives all of himself; he would never consider doing anything but his best work. He appreciates excellence, not only in himself but in others, and he is liberal with praise when he sees people outdoing themselves. Moreover, he's a passionate lover and an unabashedly sexual person.

In short, the King of Wands lives life to the fullest, rejoicing in every experience. His ardor for life defines him and inspires people to follow him. Sometimes, he can be prone to egotism, and he has to be careful not to become a petty tyrant, but joy and vitality are at the core of who he is. These are the qualities that make him worthy of being King.

PART VI

THE BIG PICTURE

16
Reading Dynamically

We have already alluded to the importance of reading the cards *together*. You don't just want to evaluate each card individually, without looking at the connections between them; rather, you want to take the tarot reading as a holistic unit, something greater than the sum of its parts. Remember, tarot is storytelling. A good story is one where the end hearkens back to the beginning, where we see the characters grow and change over the course of the narrative. All the parts of a story connect to each other; the same is true for the cards in a tarot reading.

In this chapter, we'll explore a handful of techniques that can help you draw connections between the cards and look at a reading from a more holistic point of view. These techniques aren't meant to replace individual card-by-card analysis; rather, they give you a glimpse of the bigger picture, as a complement to the details you see in each individual card. If you look only at the cards as isolated, individual units, you'll miss the forest for the trees. On the other hand, if you only use these larger techniques at the expense of interpreting the individual cards, you'll miss the trees for the forest. You want to try to maintain a healthy balance of the wider and narrower perspectives in order to give yourself the most complete possible understanding of your reading.

Suits and Elements

We've already mentioned that each suit in the Minor Arcana has an elemental association. These elemental correspondences don't only help you in understanding the themes pertaining to a particular card; when you agglomerate them, they can also give you an overview of the relevant themes in the overall reading. If a reading is dominated by one suit, that tells you that the energy of the suit is present in full force and is directly relevant to the querent's question. Conversely, if one suit is conspicuously absent from a reading, that tells you that something is lacking. Roughly speaking, the elemental significations of the suits are as follows:

- Pentacles point to the importance of work, money, health, home life, and pragmatism.
- Swords point to communication, intellect, abstract ideas, logic, and rationality.
- Cups point to the querent's emotional life, romantic and familial relationships, sensitivity, and feeling.
- Wands point to willpower, intention, creativity, sexuality, and conflict.

Looking at the suits can give you insight into hidden factors in a reading. If someone asks you for a reading about their work life but almost all the cards you pull are Cups, that tells you that their problem isn't *really* about work—it's about interpersonal relationships. The relationships in question might be the ones in the querent's workplace, but seeing the predominance of Cups indicates to you that the reading should focus on that human, emotional aspect of things rather than on the ins and outs of the specific tasks that your querent is charged to perform. If a client comes to you because they're worried about getting into art school but their reading doesn't contain a single Wand, it may well be worth asking why they want to go to art school and what they're really passionate about—as any passion they might feel is not showing through in the reading.

Although we haven't yet talked at length about the Major Arcana (see chapter 18), their disproportionate presence or absence in a reading is also noteworthy. The Minor Arcana are the "lesser mysteries" of the tarot. They reflect the themes that fill our everyday lives and the kinds of questions and experiences that most of us encounter in real, ordinary life. The Major Arcana, on the other hand, are the "greater mysteries." They represent big, universal, archetypal themes that are larger than any one person's life—big things like transformation, justice, and renewal. The Major Arcana put us in touch with something larger than ourselves, something that sits at the heart of what it is to be a human.

In a reading, then, a disproportionate number of Major Arcana signify that something *big* is going on. The majors tell you to sit up and pay attention because you're living through a defining moment in your life. Whatever the events of the reading, whatever the question you've asked, it has the potential to reshape the course of your life in a big way. Furthermore, the Major Arcana often signify that events are, in some way, out of your hands—that you're at the mercy of larger transformational forces outside of yourself. In contrast, a reading *without* the Major Arcana (or with very few) indicates that your question is fairly small in the grand scheme of things, and you have the power to influence its outcome through your direct actions.

Celtic Cross Spread

This is perhaps the most famous tarot spread in existence, and it is the one upon which the Crossroads spread from chapter 4 is based. There are a number of variations of the Celtic Cross, and you'll see different books offering slightly different interpretations for each card position, but this is the variant I use.

Begin by dealing out the first six cards exactly as you do for the Crossroads spread. Then, to the right of everything, deal out four more cards in a vertical line, starting from the bottom.

The first six cards are interpreted the same as in the Crossroads spread. The central card represents you, and the card overlaying it is what "crosses" you—the problem or situation that you're dealing with. The cards to the left and right represent the recent past and the immediate future. The bottom card is the root cause of the situation, and the top card is overall advice.

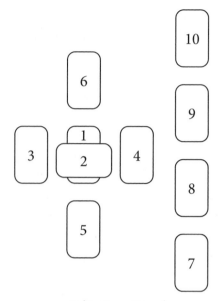

Celtic Cross Spread

The four additional cards on the right-hand side add further nuance to the reading. The card at the bottom of the column represents your perception of yourself; not you as you actually are, but the way you see yourself through your own eyes. This card—particularly when compared to the central card in the spread—can give you a bit of a reality check and help you see when your self-image is inaccurate. The next card up in the column represents external influences and other people who are relevant to your situation. Above that, the ninth card in the reading indicates your hopes and fears. It may seem odd to put these two things together in one card position, but our hopes are often mirror images of our fears, and vice versa. Finally, the card at the top of the column is a long-term outcome, a progression further into the future than the "immediate future" card you've already interpreted. Having two outcome cards allows you to see how the future develops over time, as the way things turn out in the short run is often not the same as their final development.

Practice Reading: The Celtic Cross

Perform a reading for yourself using the Celtic Cross spread. Take particular note of the distribution of the four suits and the Major Arcana in this reading. Each suit of the Minor Arcana makes up 18 percent of the tarot deck, and the majors make up 28 percent, so you'd expect to see one to two cards from each minor suit and two to three cards from the majors. If you have significantly more or less than that for any suit, think about how the elemental energy of that suit relates to the question you've asked. What elemental energy do you have a lot of? What are you lacking? And how does this inform the overall message of your reading? Record the reading in your tarot journal.

Numbers and Numerology

The suits are one axis along which the Minor Arcana share qualities in common; the numbers are another. Just as all the cards of a particular suit are held together by a shared elemental energy, the cards of a particular number are held together by a shared numerological energy. Numerology is a whole field of study in itself, but insofar as it intersects with tarot, it expresses the idea that numbers (particularly, for our interests, the numbers one through ten) can be associated with certain themes, symbols, and energies. There is a thematic commonality among all of the Aces, all of the Twos, the Threes, and so on—just as there was a commonality among all the cards of a given suit.

- Aces are about beginnings and potential.
- Twos are about duality and reciprocity.
- Threes are about dynamism and change.
- Fours are about stability and foundation.
- Fives are about hardship and strife.
- Sixes are about equilibrium and reevaluation.
- Sevens are about perspective and intention.
- Eights are about freedom and motion.
- Nines are about fulfillment and culmination.
- Tens are about consequences and endings.

Importantly, the numerological and elemental associations of the Minor Arcana aren't meant to be used as a mix-and-match shorthand for each card's meaning. It is true that the Three of Swords is about dynamism in a way, because it is a Three, and that it is about thoughts in a way, because it is a Sword; however, you'd be wildly off base to pull a card with a bloody, dripping heart on it and say, "Ah, yes, this card is about how dynamic your thoughts are." The elemental and numerological correspondences of the cards are meant to overlay and supplement the interpretation of each individual card, not to replace the interpretive process.

As with the elemental correspondences, numerology can give you a wider perspective on your reading as a whole, not just an understanding of each card on its own. If all four Eights show up in a reading, you know that your querent is yearning to be free and to move forward in their life. On the other hand, if your reading has all of the Fours, you know that your querent is concerned with stability and wants to preserve the status quo.

Personalizing Numerology

Tarot readers have subtly different ideas about what the numbers in tarot correspond to. There are broad similarities (just about everybody agrees that Aces deal with new things and Fives are a source of trouble), but the specific keywords people use will vary. As with everything in tarot, the use of numerology is personal, and the best way to go about it is to find what resonates best with you. The numerological keywords given in this book are the ones I use based on my personal understanding of the themes in the Minor Arcana, but you may want to develop your own.

This is a great exercise for your tarot journal. Pull out all four cards of a particular number (e.g., the Sevens) and lay them out side by side. Then ask yourself, *What do these four cards have in common? What energy do they share?* Write your thoughts out in your journal, and try to reduce that shared energy to one or two keywords you can use: "Sevens are about XYZ."

Once you've done this for all the numbers in the deck, look at your list of keywords. Do you notice similarities between certain numbers? For example, is there an affinity between the keywords you gave for the Threes and the keywords for the Sixes? If so, what does that tell you about the relationship between these cards? What about numbers that seem to have opposite or contrasting energies? Note all of this information down in your tarot journal. Then, spend some time thinking about how you would apply it in the context of a reading. Look back through your journal and find a past reading you've done where a numerological interpretation would have been helpful. Using your own keywords, what additional insight can you gain into the message of that reading?

Runs of Cards

When you have a run of consecutively numbered cards, take note. This is a sequence of cards that all go together. Their presence shows you a narrative through-line, a linear progression that guides the development of your reading. In particular, the first and last cards in the run are significant; they mark a starting point and an ending point for the progression being shown. These cards can tell you a lot about where your querent has been and where they're going, giving you more detail than if you'd just looked at the elemental correspondences of the suit.

For example, having a reading full of Swords tells you one thing, but having a run of Swords can tell you something far more specific. A run from the Two of Swords to the Eight of Swords tells you that your querent was faced with a major decision and is now feeling trapped by the choice they've made, whereas a run from the Ace of Swords to the Four of Swords tells you that your querent recently had a new idea but is now taking a break and not giving it much thought. Runs can give you incredibly specific information about the narrative trajectory of a reading.

You can even look for runs across multiple suits. If you have a reading with the Seven of Cups, Eight of Swords, Nine of Cups, and Ten of Wands, that's still a numerical progression taking you from the Seven to the Ten; even though the cards aren't all in the same suit, this sequence can tell you where your querent started and where they ended up. Paying attention to patterns like these is one of the best ways to bring the cards in a reading together, so that each card echoes the energy of the others.

Spread Positions

When you see connections between the cards occupying certain positions in a reading, that's a signal that those areas of the reading are connected as well. Suppose, for example, that you're doing a reading using the Heart-Shaped Relationship spread from chapter 4, and the outcome card for this reading is the Four of Cups. Less than thrilled with this outcome, you want to understand *why* the relationship is heading in that direction—and you notice that there are two other Fours present in the reading. In the "what you want" position, you have the Four of Wands; in the "what your partner needs" position, you have the Four of Pentacles.

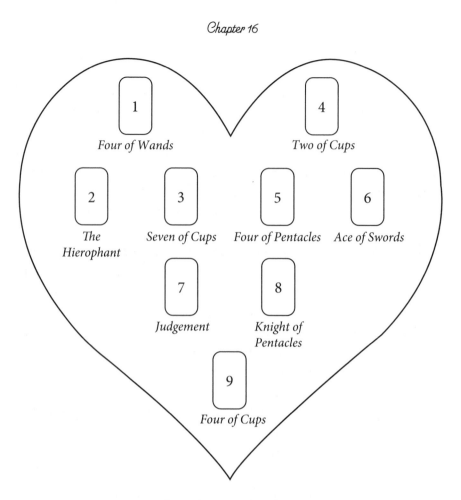

Relationship Spread With Fours

This tells you several things. First off, it shows that a desire for stability is a key theme for the reading and is connected to the ultimate (stagnant and underwhelming) outcome of the relationship. Secondly, and more interestingly, it connects that theme to what you want out of the relationship and what your partner needs. Here is the core tension of the reading: a fundamental disagreement about security and dependability, which strikes at an incompatibility between your wants and your partner's needs.

To take another example, look at the following Past/Present/Future spread. Here, we have a run of three cards: the Ace, Two, and Three of Pentacles. These three cards are building toward the Three of Pentacles (the culmination of the run). However, the run is not arranged in numerical order; the Three is at the start of the run, rather than the end, and it occupies the "past" position in the spread. This means that the energy of this reading is focused on the past. Rather than moving forward into the future, the run in this reading tells us that the querent is moving backward, regressing toward the memory of some time in the past.

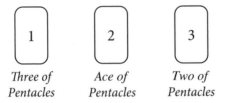

Three of   *Ace of*   *Two of*
Pentacles   *Pentacles*   *Pentacles*

Whenever you look at the relationship between the cards in a reading, think about the way those cards are situated in the structure of the overall spread. What spread positions are the cards oriented around, and what themes—both in the cards themselves and in the structural design of the spread—appear to be emphasized by the dynamic relationships you've observed?

Practice Reading: Finding Patterns

Your querent is Aliyah, a young woman who has just graduated high school and is about to start her first semester of college. She's incredibly nervous about the experience. She's worried about making friends, doesn't know what she wants her major to be, has anxiety about living far away from her family, and has impostor syndrome with regard to her academic accomplishments.

You do a reading for her to find out what her first semester of college will be like, using the Hopes and Fears spread from chapter 13. You draw the following cards:

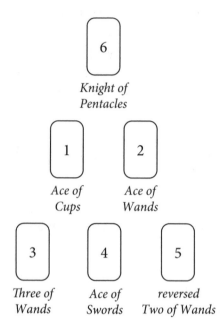

Interpret this reading for Aliyah, paying close attention to the dynamic reading techniques discussed in this chapter. Record your reading in your tarot journal.

What's Missing?

The cards that aren't present in a reading can often be just as telling as the cards that are. Take a look at the following three-card reading. What sticks out at you?

There are a couple of potential answers to that question, but the one I'm looking for is this: *The Seven of Wands is missing.* We have a run of cards from the Five through the Eight of Wands, but that run is disrupted by the absence of the Seven. This conspicuous absence tells us something important about the reading—it shows us what energy the querent doesn't have.

The querent in this reading has just come out of (and, by all appearances, won) a tough battle, and is excited to move on to bigger and better things. However, she lacks the perseverant, self-defensive energy of the Seven of Wands—and without that energy, she's potentially vulnerable. The new direction she wants to go, as symbolized by the Eight of Wands, is not guaranteed to be a success, because the reading shows that the querent might not have what it takes to stick to her guns when her plans are thwarted. This, then, is part of the advice you can give her. She needs to cultivate the energy of the Seven and bring it into her life in order to facilitate success for the Eight.

By understanding what's lacking in a reading, you can guide your querent to fill in the gaps and help make a given situation more fulfilling and balanced.

17

The Fool's Journey

When I say that tarot is storytelling, I don't merely mean that the process of reading the cards is like telling a story. I also mean that there are stories embedded in the cards themselves. We see this to a certain extent in the Minor Arcana, where each suit tells a story of its own. The Pentacles follow a project from inception to completion, the Swords follow an idea, the Cups follow a feeling, and the Wands follow a desire.

These stories are not the only stories that could be told about these themes, of course; not every new project develops into the Ten of Pentacles, and certainly not every idea ends up as ruinous as the Ten of Swords. However, these stories are woven into the fabric of tarot, and every other story we tell with the deck—every reading we perform—hearkens back to them. When you draw the Eight of Wands in a reading, you are not only interpreting this card as it stands alone, but also drawing on its position relative to the other cards in the suit of Wands and the way it relates to them. Each card's place in the story of its suit is an ineluctable part of what it means.

At long last, then, we come to the greatest story in the tarot deck: the story of the Major Arcana. The majors are the big themes of the tarot deck, representing archetypal energies and major forces that shape all of our lives. Consequently, the story of the majors is also big and universal. The minors tell smaller stories; the suit of Wands is the story of *a* desire, not of *all* desires. The majors, on the other hand, tell one story that encompasses all the others. It's the story to end all stories, a single cosmic narrative that's written into the universe itself. The Major Arcana don't just tell *a* story; they tell *the* story that structures all of our lives.

The Order of the Major Arcana

"A single cosmic narrative that's written into the universe itself" is quite a lofty claim, so let's take a moment to come back to Earth and understand the practical details of what the Major Arcana are and what story they actually tell. Remember that tarot originally developed as a trick-taking card game in late medieval Italy. The structure of the suits reflects how the game was played. The four suits of the Minor Arcana are like the suits you find in any regular deck of playing cards, and the Major Arcana were additional cards set aside as trump cards. In the course of a game of tarot, if you weren't able to play a card of the appropriate suit, you could play one of the trump cards instead to win the hand; the higher the trump, the more powerful it was in gameplay.

Thus, the Major Arcana are larger, more powerful, and more significant than the minors. The grand themes of the majors quite literally trump the smaller concerns expressed by the other cards in the tarot deck. Moreover, the majors are numbered, and the higher the number, the more expansive, universal, and transpersonal its themes are. There are twenty-two Major Arcana in a tarot deck, named and numbered as follows:

0. The Fool
I. The Magician
II. The High Priestess
III. The Empress
IV. The Emperor
V. The Hierophant
VI. The Lovers
VII. The Chariot
VIII. Strength
IX. The Hermit
X. The Wheel of Fortune

XI. Justice

XII. The Hanged Man

XIII. Death

XIV. Temperance

XV. The Devil

XVI. The Tower

XVII. The Star

XVIII. The Moon

XIX. The Sun

XX. Judgement

XXI. The World

Some decks have Strength and Justice swapped, so that Strength is number eight and Justice is number eleven. Some decks, such as those in the Thoth tradition, have alternate names for some of the Major Arcana, although the cards are still fundamentally the same despite the change in nomenclature. Otherwise, this is the standard order you'll see in just about any tarot deck.

The thing I want you to notice first about this order is that one card is at a remove. There are twenty-two Major Arcana, but they're not numbered one through twenty-two; rather, they're numbered one through twenty-one, with the Fool set apart from the rest of the sequence. The Fool is number zero, neither the first card in the sequence nor the last card, but rather existing outside the numbered order of the Major Arcana. Each of the other majors has a place in the progression, a card that it comes before and a card that it comes after; the Fool, on the other hand, is everywhere and nowhere all at once.

Before we proceed any further in our discussion of the Fool's journey, go get your own tarot deck. Pull out all the Major Arcana and lay them out on a table in front of you, in order from the Magician to the World. (Keep the Fool separate, since this card doesn't properly belong to the numbered sequence of the rest of the majors.) As we talk through the Fool's journey, refer back to the sequence of the Major Arcana in your own deck. Look at the imagery of the cards, individually and together, and think about how these images might reflect the lessons we're about to discuss. Following along with this visual aid will help you make sense of the Fool's journey, especially since you haven't yet learned the divinatory themes associated with these cards.

The Fool's Journey

The Fool is the central character of the story in the Major Arcana, the figure who moves freely through the narrative told by the other twenty-one cards. The Fool is a protean figure with the potential to be anything and everything; they exist in a constant state of becoming. The underlying story told by the majors is the story of the Fool—who could be anyone—learning the lessons of the other twenty-one cards, discovering who they are, and claiming an identity for themselves. This story is the journey from raw, untapped potential to actualization, fulfillment, and maturity.

In many ways, the Fool is the everyperson of tarot. The Fool's journey is the story of discovering oneself, and that's something that we all experience. When we look at the Fool, then, we see a reflection of ourselves. The Fool's journey is the fundamental, indelible experience of being human. The things the Fool encounters on their journey—things like love, strength, ruin, and fate—are all core to the human experience, and they are things that we must all face, sooner or later, as we try to navigate our lives. The Fool's journey is a prototype of human life, a blueprint that shows us the trials and lessons that are universal to human experience.

What, then, are those trials and lessons? They begin with the Fool's realization that there is something greater than themselves. Before beginning their journey of discovery, the Fool isn't aware that there's anything for them to discover in the first place. They think they know everything—not in a blustery, arrogant way, but in the innocent way that children are simply unaware of all the things they don't know. The Fool's journey begins with an awakening, a realization that there is something *more*, and a curiosity that drives them to want to discover it.

The Fool meets with two mysterious and magical figures, the Magician and the High Priestess. These figures show the Fool that there's something more for them to learn, some greater mystery they don't have access to. The Magician and the High Priestess equip the Fool with the tools needed to get started on their journey, pointing them in the right direction so that they can discover more on their own.

From there, the Fool looks to learn from established authority figures: the Empress, Emperor, and Hierophant (who, in some older decks, is named the Pope). These figures may be political and religious authorities, but they could also represent parents, teachers, or mentors. The key theme here is that the Fool is trying to learn from people who know more than they do, and who have some kind of clout, power, or reputation. The Fool's first instinct is to seek out people who can teach and nurture them.

But learning does not stop there; the Fool's journey also requires introspection and self-discovery that must come from within. With the Lovers, the Fool has the experience of love and of knowing themselves in relation to another. With the Chariot, the Fool discovers their own ambition and drive. With Strength, they find their innate tranquility and strength of character. And living alone on a mountaintop with the Hermit, they learn to trust their own wisdom and listen to their inner voice.

Having learned from others and learned from themselves, the Fool then has to experience the boundaries of their world; they must realize that there are some things beyond their control. The Wheel of Fortune teaches them about fate and luck, while Justice shows them that they are accountable for the way their actions affect others. After Justice, the Fool encounters the Hanged Man, who demonstrates that sometimes suffering cannot be avoided, and Death, which teaches that all things have to end eventually in order for new things to begin.

From Temperance and the Devil, the Fool learns their own virtues and vices and is confronted with the perpetual struggle between the two. When the Fool visits the Tower and sees it blasted down by lightning, they come to understand that sometimes things fall apart, and that it's not their fault when disaster strikes.

After the disaster of the Tower, the Fool finds solace by connecting to a sense of something greater than themselves—opening themselves up to communion with forces of nature like the Star, the Moon, and the Sun. The Star promises that renewal and healing are possible even after the worst catastrophes, the Moon shows the value of mysteries and dreams, and the Sun is a shining beacon of light and truth that finally guides the Fool toward their ultimate revelation.

The Fool has another great awakening with Judgement, where they finally come to understand their purpose and place in the universe. And at long last, the Fool is made one with the spirit of the World itself, completing the cycle of their journey and fulfilling their quest for discovery and self-actualization. With the World, the Fool is made whole and attains the deep knowledge that they had set out to acquire.

This is a process that we all go through over the course of our lives. We may experience the steps in a different order and encounter the themes of the cards in our own way, but we must all learn the Fool's twenty-one lessons. The story of the Fool's journey through the Major Arcana of the tarot is an allegorical representation of every human being's experience on Earth. Its symbolism is deep and universal, speaking to the greater question we all have: "Why am I here, and what am I supposed to do with my life?"

Practice Reading: Your Fool's Journey

Remove all the Major Arcana from your deck, setting the rest of the cards aside. Shuffle the Major Arcana and ask, "Where am I right now in my journey through life?" Then, draw three cards. These cards represent the archetypes of the Fool's journey that are manifesting most strongly in your life at the present moment. Pay attention to how these cards relate to each other, both thematically and sequentially. Do you see similar themes that connect to one main area of your life, or three disparate themes that each point to a different happening? Are the cards clustered in one part of the numerical sequence of the Major Arcana, or are they spread out across the whole range of trump cards? How does your personal Fool's journey compare to the one expressed by the classic numerical ordering of the Major Arcana? Record your reading in your tarot journal.

The Septenaries of the Major Arcana

Over the course of our lives, we each encounter the energies of all the cards in the Major Arcana, although we may come across those energies in a different order than the Fool does, as we experience them in our own time and in our own way. The Fool's journey is one big, all-encompassing story that contains the seeds of an infinite variety of smaller stories within itself.

One way these smaller stories manifest is in a threefold division of the twenty-one Major Arcana (excluding the Fool) into groups of seven, which are called *septenaries*. The three septenaries of the Major Arcana tell three closely related stories, each of which is a microcosm of the larger story of the Fool's journey. By looking at these smaller stories, both individually and together, we can gain a deeper insight into the larger story they comprise. The septenaries are as follows:

- The Magician, the High Priestess, the Empress, the Emperor, the Hierophant, the Lovers, and the Chariot
- Strength, the Hermit, the Wheel of Fortune, Justice, the Hanged Man, Death, and Temperance
- The Devil, the Tower, the Star, the Moon, the Sun, Judgement, and the World

This division breaks down the Fool's journey into three distinct categories. The first septenary deals with the Fool's personal psychological development. The Magician presents the Fool with a sense of personal autonomy and direction, the High Priestess shows them that there's something greater than themselves, the Empress nurtures them, the Emperor gives them order and structure, the Hierophant teaches and guides them with established wisdom, the Lovers show them their relation to other people, and the Chariot culminates the septenary by providing the Fool with a clear path forward in their personal journey. These seven cards, taken together, tell the story of a miniature Fool's journey at the individual level.

The next septenary tells a similar story, but this time at a societal level; in the second septenary, the Fool discovers not themselves, but rather the values and restrictions that structure the wider world in which they live. They're armed with Strength to face the world, and then they meet the Hermit who chooses to hide himself away from other people. From there, the Fool learns about things that affect everyone, and not just themselves: the Wheel of Fortune that turns capriciously and gives out good and bad luck to all people, the principle of Justice by which all people must live, the suffering of the Hanged Man, and the inevitable human experience of Death. Finally, the Fool learns the virtue of Temperance, which allows them to find the equilibrium necessary to navigate the world after everything they have encountered in this second septenary.

The third septenary tells a similar story again, but at an even larger scale, focusing on cosmic energies that are beyond the human world. The Fool meets the boundless appetite of the Devil and sees the unchecked chaos of the Tower; then, they progress to forces of nature like the Star, the Moon, and the Sun. These are transcendent energies, the things that make up the heavens themselves, and they are much, much larger than any of us—or even the society we inhabit. After the Sun, the Fool has a vision of the final Judgment Day. Then, at last, they come to a complete understanding of the World itself.

It's also worth your time to look at the shared qualities of cards occupying the same position across septenaries. Consider:

- The Magician, Strength, and the Devil all deal with the self. The Magician endows a sense of self-purpose, Strength gives quietude and grace, and the Devil is selfish and all-consuming.

- The High Priestess, the Hermit, and the Tower are revelations. The High Priestess initiates the Fool, the Hermit teaches the Fool to look inward, and the Tower is the shocking clarity of a lightning strike.

- The Empress, the Wheel of Fortune, and the Star respond to those revelations. The Empress helps the Fool grow, the Wheel of Fortune reminds them of things they can't control, and the Star heals them after calamity.

- The Emperor, Justice, and the Moon foreshadow who the Fool is to become. The Emperor is a vision of personal power, Justice is a commitment to equality and balance, and the Moon embraces mystery and the unconscious mind.

- The Hierophant, the Hanged Man, and the Sun show the Fool truths they hadn't seen before. The Hierophant offers traditional wisdom, the Hanged Man gives wisdom through hardship, and the Sun is the clarifying light of day.

- The Lovers, Death, and Judgement transform the Fool. The Lovers take the Fool's self and make them aware of another, Death ends one thing to begin another, and Judgement is a transmutation and awakening.

- The Chariot, Temperance, and the World are the lesson learned. The Chariot is a clear path forward, Temperance is balance and harmony, and the World is a deep understanding of the universe itself.

These three septenaries, then, divide the Fool's journey into three smaller cycles: one personal, one social, and one universal. Each of these smaller stories follows the same seven-step pattern—self, revelation, aftermath, foreshadowing, truth, transformation, and finality. On a much larger scale, this is the pattern of the Fool's development as they pursue their journey from the Magician to the World. These three stories work in harmony to tell the narrative of the Fool's quest for enlightenment at three different scales. By looking at the smaller scales, you can better understand the narrative thrust of the Fool's journey, and can then apply that insight to the Major Arcana taken as a larger unit.

Septenaries Spread

This is a larger tarot spread, and one I would only recommend for big questions dealing with major issues in your life. This spread gives you a lot of information about where you've been and where you're going, and if you use it for smaller questions, it can easily overload you. For big-picture questions about the direction your life is headed, however, this spread can give you a great sense of perspective.

On the left-hand side of your reading space, place down your significator. If you prefer not to use a significator card, you may randomly draw a card to represent you. To the right of this card, deal out twenty-one other cards, in three rows of seven. These three rows show you three septenaries of your own life. The top row deals with your development as an individual, the middle row deals with your place in society, and the bottom row deals with larger philosophical questions.

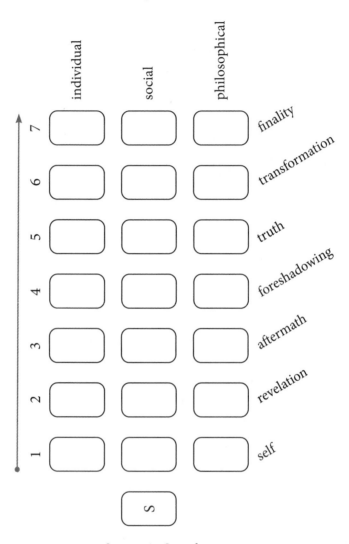

Septenaries Spread

Within each row, the cards from left to right represent the seven steps of each septenary: self, revelation, aftermath, foreshadowing, truth, transformation, and finality. Each row can show you the arc of your own personal narrative at one of the three levels represented by the septenaries. It's also a good idea to look at the rows in relation to each other—not just as three separate readings. Are there common themes among them? What do those themes say about your larger journey? Record your reading in your tarot journal.

18

The Major Arcana

Because the Major Arcana represent universally accessible themes, they are in many ways the easiest cards to understand. If you've never seen a tarot deck before and you try to give yourself a reading, you might struggle to interpret a card like the Three of Wands or the Page of Cups, but you'll at least be able to get a rough sense of the meaning of cards like Strength or Justice. The key with the Major Arcana is to look for the larger theme behind the name of the card. What is the deep, universal experience underlying each image? When you look at these cards, what about them feels like it gets at the essence of what it is to be human? Those themes, when you find them, are the deep meanings of the Major Arcana.

0. The Fool

The Fool is pure, raw potential. Like the universe before the Big Bang, the Fool contains the possibility for anything and everything. They could be anyone, if they set their mind to it; the world is laid out before them, waiting for them to make their mark on it. However, the Fool's potential has not yet been actualized. They *could* be everything, but currently they aren't anything. In the image of this card, we see the Fool with their head in the clouds, not watching where they're going—and they're about to walk off a cliff! This is a warning. The Fool can sometimes be, well, foolish. They're easily caught up in dreams about what might be or what will be, and they forget to pay attention to what actually *is*.

In a reading, the Fool represents a seed that is just starting to germinate, the beginning of something that's *so* new that you don't even really know what it is. The Fool embodies innocence, guilelessness, and wonder. They can be easily duped or led astray by their own naivety, but they are capable of truly wonderful things—things that no one, not even the Fool themselves, has even begun to imagine. When you see the Fool in a reading, watch for new beginnings and keep your mind open to possibilities you haven't considered yet.

I. The Magician

The Magician is a miracle worker. On the table in front of him, he has laid out the symbols of the four suits: a pentacle, a sword, a cup, and a wand. With these, he is the master of the four elements, and he can direct the universe to manifest his will. Above his head, we see a lemniscate: the symbol of infinity. With one hand pointed to the heavens and the other pointed to Earth, the Magician is situated as a conduit of great power.

The Magician symbolizes will, direction, and ego-consciousness, the conscious application of will to the world in order to exert the changes we want to see. One danger with the Magician is that you may overestimate your power. The Magician at his weakest is nothing more than a conjurer of cheap tricks, who deludes people into thinking he can effect real change. However, at his best, the Magician has a single-minded potency that lets him accomplish truly incredible things.

When the Magician appears in a reading, he suggests a strong sense of self, as well as the confidence and clarity that come along with it. Moreover, he brings a "make it happen" attitude to everything he does, bringing his goals to fruition and manifesting things that anyone else would have dismissed as impossible.

II. The High Priestess

The High Priestess is the guardian of higher knowledge and wisdom. She sits at the entrance to her temple, flanked by the twin pillars that guard the door; behind her is a veil decorated with pomegranates, the fruit of wisdom. In order for you to pass beyond that veil and access the secret knowledge within the temple, you must first prove yourself worthy to the High Priestess. She is an initiator, an awakener, the person who gives access to the great mysteries of life.

The High Priestess can represent secrets, mysteries, and anything that is hidden and unknown. Any truth we seek, anything that is kept behind a locked door, is in the purview of the High Priestess. Further than that, she can represent deep intuition—the things we just *know* without explanation, the knowledge that comes from some hidden place inside ourselves.

It is easy to see the High Priestess's secretiveness as exclusionary and selfish, but that's really not what it's about. Rather, the High Priestess keeps knowledge hidden because there are people who aren't yet ready to know it. People are inclined to ignore truths that they don't want to hear; the High Priestess knows this and reserves her knowledge for people who are actually open to learning from it. All things come in due time, when we're ready for them.

III. The Empress

The Empress is a warm, motherly figure. She reclines on her throne in a lush garden, surrounded by the fullness of life. This card is all about cultivation, nurturing, and growth. The Empress is like a gardener who knows exactly what conditions a seed needs in order to grow, flower, and bear fruit. She applies this same attitude in all areas of life, nurturing projects, people, relationships, investments, and the like. The energy of the Empress pours out careful time and attention to make something grow to its full potential.

In a reading, the Empress may indicate that you are on either end of this process—either the one being cared for or the one who has to do the caring. The approach represented by this card is one of kindness, attention, and a gentle touch. This card can also represent abundance, growth, and prosperity—anything that is flourishing and in its prime.

At times, the energy of the Empress can be overabundant. Unchecked, it may need to be countered with some level of severity and strictness. The Empress is not forceful or demanding; rather, she makes room for the things around her to grow and flourish, and then encourages them to come into their own. The result is a sense of vibrancy and vitality that surrounds everything she touches.

IV. The Emperor

Where the Empress was gentle and encouraging, the Emperor is a figure of strength and authority. He has a commanding, charismatic presence. This card symbolizes power, force, and the rule of law—not just at the level of government and politics, but also in all areas of life. The Emperor reminds us to keep our promises, to follow the rules, and to do the right thing. As a reflection on ourselves, the Emperor is also a reminder that we have power of our own; sometimes, we get to make the rules and demand that others follow them. The Emperor is, first and foremost, a leader, and we're able to mold ourselves in his image and become leaders in our own right.

The Emperor's power is largely personal rather than institutional; he leads because he has convinced others to follow him. Sometimes this can be a stumbling block; the Emperor can imagine that he's special and doesn't have to follow the same rules everyone else does. In a reading, the Emperor can sometimes signify this kind of exceptionalism, or—on the other end of the spectrum—a blind and unquestioning adherence to established authority. Authority is not all bad, though, and the Emperor is a skilled and devoted ruler. This card embodies order and accountability; when applied right, these are indispensable qualities in life.

V. The Hierophant

This card represents orthodoxy, conservatism, and tradition. The Hierophant is a religious leader, dressed as the Pope with acolytes prostrated before him—but more deeply than that, he is the voice of tradition. The Hierophant carries the wisdom of those who have gone before. He expresses not just religious orthodoxy, but also culture, language, and heritage. He is to be found in Great Grandma's pecan pie recipe, in the advice your mother gave you on your first day of school, and in the study of history. He keeps the flame of past knowledge alive, knowing full well that eventually someone will need it to get by.

The old ways are not always best, and the Hierophant's love of tradition can sometimes give way to stubbornness and a refusal to accept innovation. This card always represents a tendency toward conservatism and preserving what we have rather than seeking something new; when taken to the extreme, this energy can be counterproductive and limiting.

It is important, however, to keep perspective and remember the value that the Hierophant holds. In a reading, this card encourages us to look at the path others have tread and to seek help from those who are older, wiser, or more experienced than us. Not everything has to be innovated and done all by yourself.

VI. The Lovers

It is easy to look at this card and read it literally, as signifying romantic love. However, that's not the essence of what the Lovers mean. This card is bigger than just romantic love. It's about the essential relationship between self and other, the awareness that you exist dynamically in connection to other people. You depend on others and they depend on you; the profound awareness of that bond is what the Lovers are all about. At its heart, the Lovers card signifies a matched set, a perfect complement of people or things that balance each other as if they were two halves of a whole. This can manifest as romantic love, but it can also be many other things.

The Rider-Waite-Smith system shows this card with Adam and Eve in the Garden of Eden, presided over by a winged angel. Some other decks, particularly in the Tarot de Marseille tradition, depict a man choosing between two women; in these systems, the Lovers can adopt a secondary meaning of being confronted with a difficult decision, often one that forces you to choose between your head and your heart.

The Lovers teach us to find harmony and fulfillment through connection by reaching out to something beyond ourselves. The core message of this card is that you are not alone.

VII. The Chariot

The Chariot is a card of drive, ambition, and independence. The charioteer commands two sphinxes, one white and one black. These sphinxes represent forces within that are at odds with each other; each sphinx wants to pull the Chariot in a different direction. It is up to the charioteer, then, to know exactly where he wants to go and to direct the sphinxes to take him there. The Chariot shows you that you are in control of your life.

The converse of this is that when the Chariot gets out of balance, the two sphinxes start pulling in different directions, and you end up going nowhere. The negative energy of this card can indicate that you're *out* of control, being dragged around by external forces. If that's the case, it's your duty to get things under control, seize the reins, and direct your life toward the things you want—and not just what circumstances dictate.

This card represents a clarity of purpose, a vision of what you want and how to accomplish it. With the Chariot, you see your path forward; you know what your ultimate goal is, and you see the route you need to take in order to get where you're going. You have a plan, you know how to execute it, and you're taking action.

VIII. Strength

Strength is another card not to be taken too literally. This card doesn't represent physical strength, force, or intimidation; rather, it's about inner strength and strength of character. In this card, we see a young woman who has tamed a lion—not by coercing it or whipping it into submission, but with love and gentleness. She has befriended the beast, allowed herself to be vulnerable with it, and in so doing she has turned a terrifying monster into a loving companion.

This card represents inner peace and equanimity. It often speaks to a need to tame the beast within, to come to terms with the shadow side of one's own personality, to embrace and heal the wounded parts of ourselves. When we lose sight of our own strength, we feel lost, helpless, and alone. The troubles we're faced with can seem insurmountable, and we can feel exposed and at the mercy of other people. Strength reminds us that this is not the case.

True strength comes from within, and the Strength card shows us that some obstacles can be overcome not with force or strategy, but simply by finding a sense of calm and balance within ourselves. Kindness, empathy, and fortitude are the key virtues that unlock the Strength card, and that allows us—like the maiden depicted in the card—to tame the beast we face.

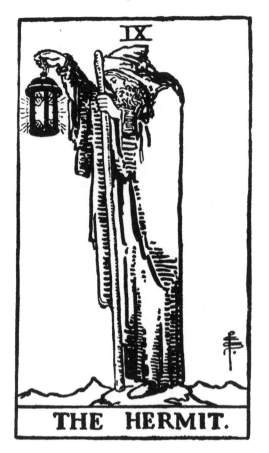

IX. The Hermit

Like Strength, the Hermit is a card of turning inward. In this case, we look inward not to find inner strength, but rather to find inner wisdom. The Hermit is a figure who isolates himself from the noise and hubbub of society so that he can seek truth and higher knowledge on his own. He lives on a mountaintop, seeing only by the light of his lifted lantern. The life of an anchorite is a potentially lonely existence, but it is a deep and fulfilling one.

The Hermit offers the sort of wisdom that can't be taught in a classroom or written down in a book. It's the quiet wisdom that only comes after spending long periods in meditation, contemplation, and introspection. It can be knowledge of yourself, or it can be a deep insight that comes from somewhere inside of you rather than from others.

Occasionally, the Hermit can represent loneliness, isolation, or an unwillingness to listen to what others have to say; this happens when the Hermit's solitude becomes unhealthy and antisocial instead of meditative. Eventually, the Hermit must come down off the mountain; this card is not about abandoning other people altogether, but about learning to hear your own inner voice so that it isn't drowned out by the voices of others.

X. The Wheel of Fortune

Fate is fickle. This is the lesson of the Wheel of Fortune, which depicts the ever-turning wheel of fate. You can have good fortune on one day and terrible luck the next; fate is impassive, impartial, and uncaring. You can never be sure what's coming your way. The same forces of fate can turn a beggar into a monarch, a criminal into a saint, and a nobody into a celebrity—or vice versa. It all depends on which way the Wheel turns.

When the Wheel of Fortune appears in a reading, it has a clear message (though often one that people don't want to hear): things are out of your control. You're subject to forces larger than you, and there are circumstances in place that you can't influence, no matter how much you might want to. You might get lucky and have things go your way, or you might get screwed over. Either way, it's out of your hands. There is nothing you can do to control the situation.

It's hard to surrender the illusion of control, but the Wheel of Fortune encourages us to do exactly that. We want to feel like we can influence the world around us, but sometimes, we're better served by accepting that there are things we cannot change and waiting to see how they turn out.

XI. Justice

The Justice card in tarot doesn't merely represent justice in the limited, human sense of a court of law—although in a reading, it certainly can point to lawyers, judges, and judicial processes. This card is, more broadly, about justice in a cosmic sense, the perpetual rebalancing of the scales of the universe. In this card, we see a woman holding scales and a sword; her scales let her measure what is needed to maintain the balance of the world, and her sword lets her cut down anyone and anything that stands in the way of that balance.

Justice, as we see it in this card, is cold and impartial. Like a judge trying to maintain objectivity, Justice is not swayed by emotional appeals or impassioned pleas; the Justice we see in this card cares only about the facts of a situation. If things are out of balance, Justice will intervene to put them to rights; if things are in balance, Justice has been done. Often, the equilibrium reached by the Justice card feels unfair to some because people can't help seeing things from their own subjective point of view. When a compromise is foisted upon us, we may feel cheated because we didn't get everything we wanted—but Justice doesn't care what we want. It only cares about what's right.

XII. The Hanged Man

The Hanged Man is one of the harder cards in the deck. Here, we see a man hanging from a tree with a noose wrapped around one leg. In this card, our worlds are—literally and figuratively—turned upside-down. The Hanged Man represents moments of suffering, confusion, and difficult trials that have to be undergone. Because of the connotation of capital punishment, the Hanged Man may also symbolize having to face the unpleasant consequences of our actions. Whatever this card brings to a reading, it's not pleasant, and it involves pain and hardship.

However, the suffering of the Hanged Man is never without purpose. Unlike with some cards in the deck, the Hanged Man always has a lesson to teach us: we suffer in order to learn. The saying "what doesn't kill you makes you stronger" isn't always true, but when the Hanged Man appears, there is something to be learned. The hardship we experience makes us stronger and wiser.

In this vein, it's important to note that the noose is around the Hanged Man's foot, not his neck—his pain is not lethal. His world has been turned upside-down, but this affords him an opportunity to view things from a new perspective, and when he eventually cuts himself loose, he'll be wiser for the experience.

XIII. Death

The Death card is easy to misinterpret because we see the skeletal rider upon a pale horse and immediately think of, well, death. In fact, this card is about endings of all kinds—not the sudden, unexpected sort of ending, but the gradual winding down of something that has run its course. When Death appears in a reading, it is time for something to come to a close.

Everything ends eventually. This is a hard lesson to learn, and we often want to cling to things and keep them going long after it's time to let them go. The Death card is an important reminder that nothing can last forever, and that's okay. It's better to enjoy a thing while it lasts and then move on when it's over.

In the background of the Death card, we see the sun rising over the horizon. This holds the secret of the card: every ending is accompanied by a beginning. Old things must end in order to make room for the new. From Death, we learn that things are cyclical. We have to clear out the things that are dead and dying in order to allow new growth, much like the process of pruning a tree. In this sense, Death is something to be celebrated—not feared—as it's actually the gateway to new life.

XIV. Temperance

Temperance is a card of union and balance. In this card, we see an angel holding two cups, pouring water from one to the other. The water doesn't fall upon the ground, but instead it flows between the cups, defying the laws of physics. On the angel's chest is an upright triangle, the alchemical symbol for fire.

Temperance is about opposites coming together and the unification of complementary pairs—fire and water, heaven (the angel) and Earth. More than that, however, Temperance is about the fusion of those opposites to create something new. It's an alchemical transformation. Two things that are completely unlike each other are brought together, and when they combine, the result is the genesis of something never before seen that combines the best of both of them.

In a reading, Temperance can represent this spiritual sense of transmutation and creation. In a more limited sense, it can also point to a need for balance, moderation, and virtue. There is, in all cases, something unearthly and heavenly about Temperance. This card encourages us to look *beyond* ourselves and the world we know to imagine something better and greater than the sum of its parts. It asks us to look at things that don't seem to belong together and to think about how they can be brought into harmony.

XV. The Devil

Where Temperance is a card of moderation, balance, and transformation, the Devil is almost the exact opposite. This card symbolizes selfishness, material appetites, and egoism. Far from signifying the literal Christian Devil, the Devil card in tarot is about our own bad impulses. This card represents the things you *want*—not in a gentle, "It would be nice if I had this" sort of way, but the bottomless, all-consuming desire that seizes you and doesn't let you go. The Devil is the sort of wanting where nothing you get is ever enough, where you always want *more*. It's about being a slave to your own passions, and in a very literal sense this card can represent addiction, debt, and greed.

Not everything about the Devil is bad, however. The key feature of this card is that it's self-oriented: the Devil prioritizes himself above all others. Sometimes that's a good thing, because we have to remember that our own needs do matter. We can't set ourselves aside completely for the sake of caring for others, and sometimes the Devil will appear in a reading as an injunction to prioritize yourself. Our appetites can be destructive when they get out of control, but appetite itself is not inherently a bad thing. Desire is a fundamental and inescapable part of being alive.

XVI. The Tower

The Tower is a ruinous card. The image on this card is quite shocking. A tower is struck by lightning and beginning to collapse, and the people within it are tossed out into the storm. This card symbolizes those moments where everything falls apart, where everything you've been working for is suddenly undone and you find yourself destitute and hopeless. The Tower occupies a place of (dis)honor alongside the Ten of Swords as one of the most feared cards in a tarot deck.

And yet, importantly, there is a reason that things fall apart. When the Tower falls, that's because it wasn't built on a strong foundation to begin with. It's tempting to think that everything was perfect before disaster struck, but that's not the case; there were deep-seated problems that went unresolved, and they would have proved ruinous sooner or later. The Tower resolves those problems in the most extreme way: by tearing everything down so that you can start over from scratch.

The disastrous events of the Tower are hard, scary, and painful—but sometimes, they are inevitable. When you're faced with intractable problems, sometimes the only thing to do is to wipe the slate clean and start over. The Tower gives you the opportunity to do exactly that. After every calamity, there is a chance to start again.

XVII. The Star

Coming off the violent upheaval of the Tower, we need to experience some peace, calm, and healing. Thankfully, this is exactly what the Star affords. In this card, a nude woman kneels at the edge of a lake, pouring water onto the earth. Her nudity here is not sexual; instead, it's a sign of innocence and openness. The Star represents renewal and rebirth, especially after some kind of hardship or trauma.

The Star does not erase trauma. She doesn't make it so that bad things never happened; she *can't* do that. What she can do, however, is heal the wounds that have been inflicted and show kindness and compassion to people in pain.

She can help people move forward and make their lives better. With the Star, things will never be exactly the way they were before, but maybe that's okay. The point of the Star is to heal your wounds, not to magically undo them. You may always carry the memory of them with you, but they don't have to define who you are.

This is the most hopeful card in the tarot deck. Even in the darkest times, the Star shines bright overhead, a beacon of hope and a promise that there is still light to be found. No matter what you've been through, the Star can see you out of it.

XVIII. The Moon

The Moon is a dreamy, intuitive, artistic card. This is a card of subjectivity, of mystery, of emotion. It tells us that some things cannot be seen and known by the cold light of day—they have to be felt and experienced. There are some truths that are intimate, personal, and subjective. The world looks different by moonlight than it does during the day, and everything is tinted silver and shrouded in mystery. The Moon in tarot represents things that are not what they appear. It is a card of dreams, fantasies, and illusions.

When the Moon appears in a reading, it tells us to look beneath the surface for the things that are hidden and unapparent about our situation. Just as the dark side of the Moon is hidden from us, this card teaches that there are some things we may never know. We have to embrace the mystery of life, and we will never have perfect certainty about our world. This card demands depth. Do not rely on appearances, it warns, because appearances can be deceptive. Rather, look for the hidden truths, the things that aren't discussed out in the open. The Moon rules over the unconscious mind, and you may also want to look for messages from your unconscious that your conscious mind hasn't yet picked up on.

XIX. The Sun

Where the Moon is subjective and dreamy, the Sun is objective and rational. Here is a card that represents truth: the shining, brilliant light of truth that illuminates everything around it. On the whole, this is a positive and joyous card, as the light of the Sun brings warmth and life to the earth. In a reading, the Sun offers clarity, insight, and understanding, showing the truth of any situation and allowing you to see things for what they really are.

However, sometimes the truth hurts. Just as looking directly into the Sun can blind us, overexposure to the energy of this card can be harsh and disillusioning. Sometimes, we learn the truth about a situation only to discover that we would have preferred to be kept in the dark. With the Sun, it's important to make sure that you only ask for the truth if you're really sure you want to hear it—because once you know something, there is no going back.

Other than truth, clarity, and objectivity, the Sun can also represent a sort of youthful exuberance. The central figure on this card is a child riding a white horse, and the Sun can signify the joy of childlike play. This is a card of joy, and most of the time when it appears in a reading, it signifies happiness and good things to come.

XX. Judgement

This card is an awakening. In it, we see a depiction of the Christian Judgment Day, when the dead are called forth from their graves to ascend to the kingdom of heaven. Setting aside the religious overtones of the card's imagery, Judgement is about the feeling of having your eyes opened and being made aware of something you'd never seen before. It's a revelation.

The awakening represented by Judgement can take many forms. It's a radical, revolutionary shift in perspective, when you suddenly see the world in a completely different way. It's the aha moment of the inventor, the artist's flash of inspiration, and the class in college that changes a student's life. It's a turning point in life, such that everything that follows it is shaped and defined by this one crucial moment.

In a reading, Judgement may represent change on a smaller scale, but it still shows that things are developing in a sudden, unexpected way. With Judgement, events take a new course that no one could have predicted—and once they do, there's no going back to how they were before. This is a transformative card that ushers in a new eon; when we have a Judgement experience, we don't know exactly what will follow it, but our one guarantee is that it will be unlike anything we've seen before.

XXI. The World

The final card of the Major Arcana is the World. Here, we see a figure draped in silk, framed in the center of a wreath. As the culmination of the Major Arcana, the World is a card of completion, fruition, and fulfillment. This is the "happily ever after" card, the card that promises everything will finally be wrapped up. Every i will be dotted, every t will be crossed, and there will be no loose threads. The World offers resolution.

Nothing in tarot ever really ends. Tarot is cyclical; when one thing comes to a close, another is getting ready to begin. The wreath surrounding the central figure in the World forms a giant zero—the number of the Fool. Thus, as we come to the end of the Fool's journey and complete the cycle of the Major

Arcana, we have a hint that the cycle is about to begin all over again; the World leads us to the Fool just as surely as the Fool led us to the Magician.

In a reading, then, the World symbolizes the fruition of one thing and the seed of another. It promises completion, but it also asks us to think about what new journeys we're ready to embark on. Celebrate your achievements, but also look to the horizon and think about what comes next.

Conclusion

Congratulations! You have made it to the end of this book. By this point, you know how to read a tarot card individually or in connection to others, as well as how to use multi-card spreads, significators, and reversals. You've learned how to tap into your intuition, how to read the cards through their imagery, and how to use more analytical techniques for interpretation. We've talked about reading for yourself, for strangers, and for close friends and family. We've discussed how to remain objective in a tarot reading and how to learn from your past mistakes. You've learned all the core techniques of tarot, and if you've been following along with the practice readings, you have a fair amount of experience under your belt by now.

Now, the question arises: where do you go from here?

Advanced Tarot

Reading tarot is a lifelong enterprise. There is always more to discover about the cards. Throughout your lifetime, you will find aspects of the cards you hadn't seen before, learn new ways to interpret them, and recognize their energy in your everyday life. This book has helped you lay the foundation for a reading practice. Now you have the rest of your life to build on that foundation and create a relationship with tarot that is uniquely yours. There are a variety of ways to further develop your study of tarot; here are just a few ideas.

Try New Decks

Once you are familiar and comfortable with the imagery of your current tarot deck, you might want to branch out and try reading with a different deck. The change in imagery and art style will give you a different artist's perspective on the cards, and it will help you see them in ways you previously hadn't. Remember, no one person has a monopoly on tarot. Different artists will present the themes of the cards in different ways, and if you expose yourself to myriad depictions, you'll eventually find that some of those depictions capture an aspect of the cards you had never considered. This can help enrich you as a reader, giving you fresh ideas about the cards and keeping you from falling into an interpretive rut.

To take this one step further, it could be worthwhile to branch out and try reading with a deck from a different school than the one you're used to. If you've been using a Rider-Waite-Smith style deck, experiment with a Tarot de Marseille or a Thoth deck. All three are tarot at their core, and they share a great deal in common, but learning about the differences between them can flesh out your understanding of the cards. You may find that when you're reading with a Thoth-style deck, an insight from working with the Tarot de Marseille comes in handy, or vice versa.

Try Meditation and Pathworking

One way to deepen your relationship with the cards is to meditate on each card individually. Choose a card that you wish to work with; pull it out from your deck and study it visually. Try to commit every detail to memory, so you can close your eyes and picture it in your mind's eye. If you have aphantasia (the inability to visualize), not to worry; just memorize the details of the card so that you can describe the card accurately even when you're not looking at it.

Once you've gained this level of familiarity with the card, you can try a meditative technique known as *pathworking*. In pathworking, you visualize yourself entering the image depicted in a tarot card. See yourself walking through that landscape and meeting with the figures depicted therein. What might they say to you when you met them? What would you say in return? If there are prominent objects or animals drawn into the card, how might you interact with them? Let your imagination run wild, and allow the scene to play out in your head. Once again, if you have aphantasia, this isn't a problem; rather than trying to visualize the scene, you can just mentally talk through the sequence of events that would likely happen, taking note of who would say and do what.

Once your mental foray into the tarot card is complete, write down the whole narrative in your tarot journal. Then, take some time to reflect on the story you've just told. How does it relate to the theme of the card? Is there anything about it that's surprising or unexpected to you? Has it given you some new insight into the card that you might use in the context of a reading? Write these thoughts down in your journal as well.

Explore Other Systems

Several decks explicitly connect the seventy-eight cards of the tarot to other esoteric or divinatory systems, such as astrology or Qabalah. If you are already familiar with one of these systems, then it may behoove you to try reading with a deck that connects that system to the tarot; that way, you will be able to draw on your existing body of knowledge in order to provide fresh insight into the tarot cards. Conversely, you may use tarot as a point of entry to help yourself learn a new system.

Create Tarot Art

If you consider yourself a creative person—and even if you don't!—you can try making artworks inspired by any or all of the seventy-eight tarot cards. This art can take any form and be in any medium: a painting, a short story, a sculpture, an interpretive dance, or even a stick figure drawing. Don't allow self-consciousness about your artistic skills to prevent you from expressing yourself; the goal of this sort of exercise is not to get your work on exhibit at the Louvre (although if you do manage that, hats off to you). This exercise is about finding expression for yourself through tarot. Allow yourself to freely and creatively explore the cards in an unconventional way. Your artwork doesn't have to be good, and no one else ever has to see it if you don't want them to. It just has to be *yours*.

Part of the purpose of doing tarot-related artwork is to use a different part of your brain. Reading books about tarot is an important and valuable way to learn, but it's also by nature a thought-based, analytical form of pedagogy. Artwork is intuitive and nonrational; it is felt rather than thought. Allowing yourself to be creative with tarot will help you unlock intuitive connections that your rational mind wouldn't have found on its own, and these intuitive insights are what make your work as a tarot reader uniquely you.

Find Connections

Now that you're familiar with each of the cards individually, you can continue the process of looking for deeper thematic connections between them. Are there certain cards in the tarot deck that seem to fit together? Are there cards that are thematically very similar, such that they express different facets of the same central idea? In a similar vein, which cards feel like they complement or balance each other out? Is there any card that fills a need expressed by another, or that makes up for a lack that another card expresses? If so, what would it mean to find these cards together in a reading?

Exploring these deep connections between the cards will allow you to continue to build a rich, dynamic tarot practice—one where every reading is its own story, rather than just a copy and paste of the interpretations assigned to individual cards. Continue to reflect on the ways that the cards interact with and affect each other. I promise, you won't run out of food for thought. Try drawing two or three cards at random, and then take some time to write in your tarot journal about what these cards have in common and how they relate to each other.

Keep Reading

Finally, the single most important thing you can do to continue to strengthen your tarot practice is to read, read, read. Keep reading tarot as often as you can, for yourself and others. Do readings for as many different kinds of questions, big and small, as you can get your hands on. Experiment, make mistakes, learn from your mistakes, and keep pushing forward. Remember that tarot, like everything else, is a skill that you get better at with practice. The best way to become a master tarot reader is to practice reading tarot over and over again.

Practice Reading: What Comes Next?

Separate your deck into six piles: one for each suit of the Minor Arcana (Ace through Ten), one for the court cards, and one for the Major Arcana. Shuffle the piles and ask, "What is the next step for me in my tenure as a tarot reader?" Then, draw one card from each pile. These six cards tell you what comes next for your tarot journey. Try not to interpret them merely as six separate lessons to be learned; rather, look for the thematic through-line that unites them. If all six cards are pointing to only one thing as your next step, what would that step be?

A Final Word

I hope that your journey with tarot does not end here. I hope you continue to read the cards, to explore the mysteries they contain, and to develop a passion for tarot that will last your whole life. If we think of being a tarot reader in terms of the Fool's journey, then reading your first tarot book is only the beginning of that journey. While reading this book, you have been like the Fool encountering the Magician; this book has given you the basic tools you need in order to go out into the world as a tarot reader, and it has awakened you to the possibilities that lay ahead of you. Just as the Fool must eventually leave the Magician behind, it is now time for you and me to part ways, and for you to continue the rest of your tarot journey without me.

You may still feel trepidatious about calling yourself a tarot reader, and you may worry that there's still a great deal you don't know, but I promise you, that's okay. You already know far more than you think you do, and you have all the basic tools you need in order to become a skilled reader. All that's left is to keep reading, and to allow time and experience to do their job. I hope that by this point in the book, you have already made mistakes in tarot readings; I promise, you will make many more. Your mistakes are lessons to be learned along the way, and if you greet them with humility and sincerity, you will learn far more from experience than any book can ever teach you.

It has been a privilege to walk this portion of your path alongside you. There's a long and exciting journey ahead of you as you continue to discover the wonder of tarot. May we meet again at the end of the road, when the cycle is complete and the Fool begins their journey once more.

To Write to the Author

If you wish to contact the author or would like more information about this book, please write to the author in care of Llewellyn Worldwide Ltd. and we will forward your request. Both the author and publisher appreciate hearing from you and learning of your enjoyment of this book and how it has helped you. Llewellyn Worldwide Ltd. cannot guarantee that every letter written to the author can be answered, but all will be forwarded. Please write to:

Jack Chanek
℅ Llewellyn Worldwide
2143 Wooddale Drive
Woodbury, MN 55125-2989
Please enclose a self-addressed stamped envelope for reply,
or $1.00 to cover costs. If outside the U.S.A., enclose
an international postal reply coupon.

Many of Llewellyn's authors have websites with additional information and resources. For more information, please visit our website at http://www.llewellyn.com.

Notes

Notes

Notes